Cambridge
First Certificate
in English
4

WITH ANSWERS

Official examination papers from University of Cambridge ESOL Examinations

CAMBRIDGE UNIVERSITY PRESS
Cambridge, New York, Melbourne, Madrid, Cape Town,
Singapore, São Paulo, Delhi, Tokyo, Mexico City

Cambridge University Press
The Edinburgh Building, Cambridge CB2 8RU, UK

www.cambridge.org
Information on this title: www.cambridge.org/9780521156943

© Cambridge University Press 2010

It is normally necessary for written permission for copying to be obtained *in advance* from a publisher. The candidate answer sheets at the back of this book are designed to be copied and distributed in class. The normal requirements are waived here and it is not necessary to write to Cambridge University Press for permission for an individual teacher to make copies for use within his or her own classroom. Only those pages which carry the wording '© UCLES 2010 Photocopiable' may be copied.

First published 2010
Reprinted 2011

Printed in the United Kingdom at the University Press, Cambridge

A catalogue record for this book is available from the British Library

ISBN 978-0-521-156936 Student's Book without answers
ISBN 978-0-521-156943 Student's Book with answers
ISBN 978-0-521-156967 Set of 2 Audio CDs
ISBN 978-0-521-156974 Self-study Pack

Cambridge University Press has no responsibility for the persistence or accuracy of URLs for external or third-party internet websites referred to in this publication, and does not guarantee that any content on such websites is, or will remain, accurate or appropriate. Information regarding prices, travel timetables and other factual information given in this work is correct at the time of first printing but Cambridge University Press does not guarantee the accuracy of such information thereafter.

Contents

Thanks and acknowledgements *4*

Introduction *5*

Test 1	Paper 1	Reading	*8*
	Paper 2	Writing	*14*
	Paper 3	Use of English	*16*
	Paper 4	Listening	*22*
	Paper 5	Speaking	*28*
Test 2	Paper 1	Reading	*30*
	Paper 2	Writing	*36*
	Paper 3	Use of English	*38*
	Paper 4	Listening	*44*
	Paper 5	Speaking	*50*
Test 3	Paper 1	Reading	*52*
	Paper 2	Writing	*58*
	Paper 3	Use of English	*60*
	Paper 4	Listening	*66*
	Paper 5	Speaking	*72*
Test 4	Paper 1	Reading	*74*
	Paper 2	Writing	*80*
	Paper 3	Use of English	*82*
	Paper 4	Listening	*88*
	Paper 5	Speaking	*94*
Test 1	Paper 5 frames		*95*
Test 2	Paper 5 frames		*98*
Test 3	Paper 5 frames		*101*
Test 4	Paper 5 frames		*104*

Marks and results *107*

Test 1	Key and transcript	*116*
Test 2	Key and transcript	*130*
Test 3	Key and transcript	*144*
Test 4	Key and transcript	*157*

Visual materials for Paper 5 *colour section*

Sample answer sheets *171*

Thanks and acknowledgements

The authors and publishers acknowledge the following sources of copyright material and are grateful for the permissions granted. While every effort has been made, it has not always been possible to identify the sources of all the material used, or to trace all copyright holders. If any omissions are brought to our notice, we will be happy to include the appropriate acknowledgements on reprinting.

p. 10: The Times, © The Times Newspapers Limited 2002, nisyndication.com; p. 13: © Telegraph Media Group Limited, 2001; p. 30: Extract taken from 'Not One of Us' by June Thewson; p. 32: Syndicated from BBC Wildlife Magazine; p. 35: The Guardian for the article 'Taking Off' by Thomas Irvin, © Guardian News & Media Ltd 2001; p. 52: Extract taken from Pixie by Kate Grenville, published by Pan MacMillan; p. 54: Daily Mail; p. 74: Janet Horwood; p. 76: © Telegraph Media Group Limited, 2000; p. 79: The Times, © The Times Newspapers Limited 2005, nisyndication.com.

Colour section

p. 36: Getty Images/David Noton; p. 46: Suzi Eszterhas/Minden Pictures/FLPA; p. 68: Imagebroker/FLPA; p. C1, photo 1A: © Greg Balfour Evans / Alamy; p. C1, photo 1B: © Phil Schermeister/CORBIS; p. C2, photo 1E.1; © Sally and Richard Greenhill / Alamy; p. C2, photo 1E.2: © I Love Images / Alamy; p. C2, photo 1E.3 and p. C4, photo 1C: Reproduced by permission of Cambridge ESOL; p. C2, photo 1E.4: © blickwinkel / Alamy; p. C3, photo 1E.5: © Golden Pixels LLC / Alamy; p. C3, photo 1E.6: iStock/© Danny Warren; p. C3, photo 1E.7: © Kevin Moore / Alamy; p. C3, photo 1E.8: iStock/© Mark Goddard; p. C4, photo 1D: © Oscar Elias / Alamy; p. C5, photo 2A: © Stephen Saks Photography / Alamy; p. C5, photo 2B: © Ted Foxx / Alamy; p. C6, 2E.1: © Wave Royalty Free / Alamy; p. C6, photo 2E.2: © Chad Ehlers / Alamy; p. C7, photo 2E.3: © Henry Westheim Photography / Alamy; p. C6, photo 2E.4: © PhotoAlto / Alamy; p. C7, photo 2E.5: © Jeff Greenberg / Alamy; p. C7, photo 2E.6: iStock/© Stephan Zabel; p. C6, photo 2E.7: © ICP / Alamy; p. C8, photo 2C: © Cultura / Alamy; p. C8, photo 2D: Getty Images; p. C9, photo 3A: Getty Images/Matthias Tunger; p. C9, photo 3B: Getty Images/Antenna; p. C12, photo 3C: Getty Images/Dave & Les Jacobs; p. C12, photo 3D: © Werner Dieterich / Alamy; p. C13, photo 4A: Jon Feingersh Photography/Superstock; p. C13, photo 4B: © Alex Segre / Alamy; p. C14, photo 4E.1: © OJO Images Ltd / Alamy; p. C14, photo 4E.2: Shutterstock/Elena Elisseeva; p. C14, photo 4E.3: © Peter Titmuss / Alamy; p. C14, photo 4E.4: Getty Images/ John Foxx; p. C15, photo 4E.5: Shutterstock/Julia Pivovarova; p. C15, photo 4E.6: © Ian Shaw / Alamy; p. C15, photo 4E.7: © Adrian Sherratt / Alamy; p. C16, photo 4C: Shutterstock/Kosarev Alexander; p. C16, photo 4D: © Paul Prescott / Alamy.

Picture research by Diane Jones

Design concept by Peter Ducker

Cover design by David Lawton

The recordings which accompany this book were made at dsound, London.

Introduction

This collection of four complete practice tests comprises papers from the University of Cambridge ESOL Examinations First Certificate in English (FCE) examination; students can practise these tests on their own or with the help of a teacher.

The FCE examination is part of a suite of general English examinations produced by Cambridge ESOL. This suite consists of five examinations that have similar characteristics but are designed for different levels of English language ability. Within the five levels, FCE is at Level B2 in the Council of Europe's *Common European Framework of Reference for Languages: Learning, teaching, assessment*. It has also been accredited by the Qualifications and Curriculum Authority in the UK as a Level 1 ESOL certificate in the National Qualifications Framework. The FCE examination is widely recognised in commerce and industry and in individual university faculties and other educational institutions.

Examination	Council of Europe Framework Level	UK National Qualifications Framework Level
CPE Certificate of Proficiency in English	C2	3
CAE Certificate in Advanced English	C1	2
FCE First Certificate in English	B2	1
PET Preliminary English Test	B1	Entry 3
KET Key English Test	A2	Entry 2

Further information

The information contained in this practice book is designed to be an overview of the exam. For a full description of all of the above exams, including information about task types, testing focus and preparation, please see the relevant handbooks which can be obtained from Cambridge ESOL at the address below or from the website at: www.CambridgeESOL.org

University of Cambridge ESOL Examinations
1 Hills Road
Cambridge CB1 2EU
United Kingdom

Telephone: +44 1223 553997
Fax: +44 1223 553621
e-mail: ESOLHelpdesk@ucles.org.uk

Introduction

The structure of FCE: an overview

The FCE examination consists of five papers.

Paper 1   Reading   1 hour
This paper consists of **three parts**, each containing a text and some questions. Part 3 may contain two or more shorter related texts. There are **30 questions** in total, including multiple-choice, gapped-text and multiple-matching questions.

Paper 2   Writing   1 hour 20 minutes
This paper consists of **two parts** which carry equal marks. In Part 1, which is **compulsory**, candidates have to write either a letter or an email of between 120 and 150 words. In Part 2, there are four tasks from which candidates **choose one** to write about. The range of tasks from which questions may be drawn includes an article, an essay, a letter, a report, a review and a short story. The last question is based on the set books. These books remain on the list for two years. Look on the website or contact the Cambridge ESOL Local Secretary in your area for the up-to-date list of set books. The question on the set books has two options, from which candidates **choose one** to write about. In this part, candidates have to write between 120 and 180 words.

Paper 3   Use of English   45 minutes
This paper consists of **four parts** and tests control of English grammar and vocabulary. There are **42 questions** in total. The tasks include gap-filling exercises, word formation and sentence transformation.

Paper 4   Listening   40 minutes (approximately)
This paper consists of **four parts**. Each part contains a recorded text or texts and some questions, including multiple-choice, sentence completion and multiple-matching. Each text is heard twice. There is a total of **30 questions**.

Paper 5   Speaking   14 minutes
This paper consists of **four parts**. The standard test format is two candidates and two examiners. One examiner takes part in the conversation while the other examiner listens. Both examiners give marks. Candidates will be given photographs and other visual and written material to look at and talk about. Sometimes candidates will talk with the other candidate, sometimes with the examiner, and sometimes with both.

Grading

The overall FCE grade is based on the total score gained in all five papers. Each paper is weighted to 40 marks. Therefore, the five FCE papers total 200 marks after weighting. It is not necessary to achieve a satisfactory level in all five papers in order to pass the examination. Certificates are given to candidates who pass the examination with grade A, B or C. A is the highest. D and E are failing grades. All candidates are sent a Statement of Results which includes a graphical profile of their performance in each paper and shows their relative performance in each one.

For further information on grading and results, go to the website (see page 5).

Test 1

Test 1

PAPER 1 READING (1 hour)

Part 1

You are going to read an article about a London tour guide. For questions **1–8**, choose the answer (**A**, **B**, **C** or **D**) which you think fits best according to the text.

Mark your answers **on the separate answer sheet**.

The best kind of know-it-all

There is an art to being a good tour guide and Martin Priestly knows what it is.

It's obvious that the best way to explore a city is with a friend who is courteous, humorous, intelligent and – this is essential – extremely well-informed. Failing that, and if it is London you are visiting, then the next best thing may well be Martin Priestly, former university lecturer, now a guide, who seems to bring together most of the necessary virtues and who will probably become a friend as well.

Last spring, I took a trip around London with him, along with a party of Indian journalists. Accustomed to guides who are occasionally excellent but who often turn out to be arrogant, repetitive and sometimes bossy, I was so struck by Priestly's performance that I sought him out again to see, if I could, just how the trick was done.

This time the tour was for a party of foreign students, aged anything between 20 and 60, who were here to improve their English, which was already more than passable. As the 'tourists' gathered, Martin welcomed them with a kind of dazzled pleasure, as if he had been waiting for them with excitement and a touch of anxiety, now thankfully relieved. I have to say, all this seemed absolutely genuine.

Then we got on the coach and we were off. Martin sat in front, not in the low-level guide's seat, but up with the group, constantly turning round to make eye contact, to see if they understood him. Soon we're in a place called Bloomsbury, famous among writers in the early 20th century. 'Bloomsbury is famous for brains,' says Martin, getting into his stride. 'It's a very clever place. It's not very fashionable but it's *very* clever.' Soon after, we pass the British Museum and Bedford Square, 'a great architectural showpiece', advises Martin. The comment prompted questions which led to a conversation about building, the part played by wealthy people and how big chunks of London still belonged to them – an issue which was to re-emerge later. This was how he liked to work: themes, introduced as if spontaneously, were laid down for subsequent discussion.

Suddenly the coach stopped and it was over, two and a half hours of non-stop performance, with information, observation and humour. Martin says encouragingly, 'I do hope you enjoy London.'

We go to a nearby café to talk. Why, I asked, had he become a guide? 'Well, I used to organise a lot of courses at the university I worked for. It was quite stressful. But I had shown students around London and I enjoyed that. It seemed an obvious move to make. I did the London Tourist Board's Blue Badge course – two evenings a week for two years. That was tough, especially the exam in what is known as "coaching". You're taught to smile but everybody had difficulty with that in the exam, when you have other things to worry about. You have to do it backwards in the coach, desperately casting your eyes about to see what is coming next, and you're facing the tutors and the other trainees. *line 50*

'And you have to know so much to guide well, different places, all kinds of architecture, agriculture. What if somebody asks a question about a crop beside the road? But some of it sticks, you know . . . eventually.' He also tells me he keeps himself up to date with radio, TV and newspapers. *line 66*

There are several hundred other guides out there, all looking for a share of the work. I think, as we talk, that I am starting to understand why good guides are so rare. It's a great deal harder than it looks, and it demands, for every stretch of road, an even longer stretch of study and forethought.

8

Paper 1 Reading

1 What do we learn about Martin in the first paragraph?
    A He has two educational roles.
    B He is a colleague of the writer.
    C His job is an extension of his hobby.
    D His job suits his personality.

2 The writer decided to meet Martin again to find out how he managed to
    A win custom from other tour guides.
    B entertain large and varied tour groups.
    C avoid the failings of many other tour guides.
    D encourage people to go back to him for another tour.

3 The writer notes that on meeting the tour group, Martin
    A greeted everyone warmly.
    B seemed as nervous as everyone else.
    C praised everyone for their prompt arrival.
    D checked that everyone could understand him.

4 Martin's approach to guiding is to
    A begin with the oldest buildings.
    B encourage tourist participation.
    C move around the coach as he talks.
    D find out how much visitors know first.

5 What does 'It' in line 50 refer to?
    A showing students around London
    B performing in front of a group
    C becoming a guide
    D arranging courses

6 Martin says that the 'coaching' exam is difficult because
    A there is so much to think about.
    B you have to smile in different ways.
    C it has so many sections.
    D you have to cover different routes.

7 In lines 66–67, what does 'some of it sticks' mean?
    A Some facts are up to date.
    B Some information is remembered.
    C Some questions are answered.
    D Some lessons are revised.

8 In the last paragraph, the writer says he is impressed by
    A the distances Martin covers on his tours.
    B the quantity of work available for tour guides.
    C the amount of preparation involved in Martin's job.
    D the variety of approaches taken to guiding.

Part 2

You are going to read an article about a cookery course for children. Seven sentences have been removed from the article. Choose from the sentences **A–H** the one which fits each gap (**9–15**). There is one extra sentence which you do not need to use.

Mark your answers **on the separate answer sheet**.

The little chefs

Hilary Rose travels to Dorset, in the south of England, to investigate a cookery course for children.

There must be something in the air in Dorset, because the last place you'd expect to find children during the summer holidays is in the kitchen. Yet in a farmhouse, deep in the English countryside, that's exactly where they are – on a cookery course designed especially for children.

It's all the idea of Anna Wilson, who wants to educate young children about cooking and eating in a healthy way. 'I'm very keen to plant the idea in their heads that food doesn't grow on supermarket shelves,' she explains. 'The course is all about making food fun and enjoyable.' She thinks that eight is the perfect age to start teaching children to cook, because at that age they are always hungry. **9**

These children are certainly all smiles as they arrive at the country farmhouse. Three girls and four boys aged from ten to thirteen make up the group. They are immediately given a tour of what will be 'home' for the next 48 hours. **10** But one thing is quite clear – they all have a genuine interest in food and learning how to cook.

Anna has worked as a chef in all sorts of situations and has even cooked for the crew of a racing yacht, in limited space and difficult weather conditions. **11** 'Kids are easy to teach,' she insists, 'because they're naturally curious and if you treat them like adults they listen to you.'

Back in the kitchen, Anna is giving the introductory talk, including advice on keeping hands clean, and being careful around hot ovens. **12** Judging by the eager looks on their young faces as they watch Anna's demonstration, they are just keen to start cooking.

The children learn the simplest way, by watching and then doing it themselves. They gather round as Anna chops an onion for the first evening meal. Then the boys compete with each other to chop their onions as fast as possible, while the girls work carefully, concentrating on being neat. **13** When they learn to make bread, the girls knead the dough with their hands competently, while the boys punch it into the board, cheerfully hitting the table with their fists.

The following morning, four boys with dark shadows under their eyes stumble into the kitchen at 8.30 a.m. to learn how to make breakfast (sausages and eggs, and fruit drinks made with yoghurt and honey). We learn later that they didn't stop talking until 4.30 a.m. **14** Ignoring this, Anna brightly continues trying to persuade everyone that fruit drinks are just as interesting as sausages and eggs.

Anna has great plans for the courses and is reluctant to lower her standards in any way, even though her students are so young. **15** 'And I like to keep the course fees down,' Anna adds, 'because if the children enjoy it and go on to teach their own children to cook, I feel it's worth it.' If this course doesn't inspire them to cook, nothing will.

A This is followed by a session on 'knife skills', which will be important later on.

B She always uses top-quality ingredients, such as the best cuts of meat and the finest cheeses, so there's clearly no profit motive in this operation.

C As they wander round, they argue light-heartedly about who has had the most experience in the kitchen.

D In the garden, they learn about the herbs that they will use in their cooking.

E Their obvious tiredness may explain why one of them goes about the task so carelessly that the ingredients end up on the floor.

F This is particularly true of young boys, who are happy to do anything that will end in a meal.

G As a result, she has a very relaxed attitude to cooking, constantly encouraging the children and never talking down to them.

H This contrast will become something of a theme during the course.

Test 1

Part 3

You are going to read a magazine article about people who make short films. For questions **16–30**, choose from the options (**A–D**). The options may be chosen more than once.

Mark your answers **on the separate answer sheet**.

Which film-makers

produced a short film at a very busy time in their lives?	16
are realistic about their future together?	17
mention the need to keep on working hard at producing short films?	18
made early career decisions that would lead them towards film-making?	19
gained financial assistance after impressing an organisation in the film world?	20
like variety in their working lives?	21
have benefited from observing professional film-makers at work?	22
were not concerned by the fact that nobody recognised them?	23
suddenly realised the great potential of their film?	24
felt their studies were not providing them with what they wanted?	25
now have a reputation for excellence which can put pressure on them?	26

Which film

was considered unlucky not to receive a prize?	27
was used for a different purpose from most short films?	28
has a lot of people acting in it?	29
was completed only at the very last minute?	30

A short cut to Hollywood

We meet the most successful young makers of short films in Britain. These short films usually last no more than ten minutes and are often shown before the main films in cinemas.

A Kevin Teller and Justin O'Brien
Jumping Gerald

Anyone who saw *Together*, the surprise arthouse hit, will have been as charmed by *Jumping Gerald*, the short film which ran before it, as they were by the main feature film itself. Yet Gerald's creators faced financial difficulties from the start, and the final version wasn't even finished until the eve of its first screening. As they sat in the cinema watching it for the first time, it dawned on Teller and O'Brien just what they had achieved. 'The way people were laughing,' Teller remembers, 'we knew we were on to a good thing.' *Jumping Gerald* was nominated for Best Short Film at the British Film Festival; although it missed out on the award, it was thought by many to have deserved it. The two men are presently involved in their second production. 'We make a good team,' Teller says, 'and we'll continue to work as one. Unless, of course, one of us gets an offer he can't refuse.'

B The Collins brothers
Oh Josephine!

Tim and Mark Collins first fell in love with the art of film-making when they were young boys. Their father was often abroad on business, and his two sons would send him video diaries to inform him of the goings-on at home. Several years later, their first short film was lucky ever to get made. At the time, Tim was writing a novel between takes, and Mark was preparing to get married. *Oh Josephine!* was made with a cast of hundreds for just £500, but it went on to win several video awards nevertheless. The film really began to get the brothers noticed, and several others followed, all exceptionally well received. The brothers now feel ready to move into full-length feature films, and are busy writing a screenplay. The only disadvantage of having had such a perfect start to their careers is the weight of expectations: they have to keep coming up with the goods.

C Brian Radley and Nicky Tomlinson
More Cake Please

Radley and Tomlinson's very first short film, *More Cake Please*, was nominated for a prestigious award at the Cannes Film Festival. Tomlinson says, 'We couldn't believe it when we found ourselves on a red carpet at Cannes. No one knew who on earth we were, but that couldn't have mattered less.' Although *More Cake Please* didn't win, Radley and Tomlinson were sufficiently encouraged by the nominations to enter the film into Channel Four's short film competition at the British Film Festival. To their surprise it won, and their film-making career began to look even better with Channel Four's promise to fund their next project. The duo had chosen university courses – in media and drama – with a film-making future in mind but, disenchanted with the theoretical rather than practical experience of the industry that was provided, both men left university before completing their courses and went to work for production companies in London. They place enormous value on the hands-on experience that their work on film sets provided them with. 'We've seen so many directors get it wrong, that we kind of know how to get it right,' says Radley.

D Hiroko Katsue and Mica Stevlovsky
The Big One

Katsue and Stevlovsky speak fondly of the days when every feature film at the cinema was preceded by a short film. Katsue and Stevlovsky's short-film-making debut, *The Big One*, was rather unusual, as it became the cinema advertisement for *Big Issue* magazine. It won award after award. 'Winning a festival is great in that it raises your profile, but it doesn't mean you can rest on your laurels,' says Stevlovsky. 'Right, you can't just expect things to happen for you,' echoes Katsue. 'You could spend years going around festivals with the same old film, but we're not into that. We're always looking for different sorts of projects, never standing still. Even when we're lying on a beach on holiday, we both have ideas churning around in our heads.'

Test 1

PAPER 2 WRITING (1 hour 20 minutes)

Part 1

You **must** answer this question. Write your answer in **120–150** words in an appropriate style.

1   You have arranged to visit your English-speaking friend, Chris, for the weekend. Read Chris's letter and the notes you have made. Then write a letter to Chris using **all** your notes.

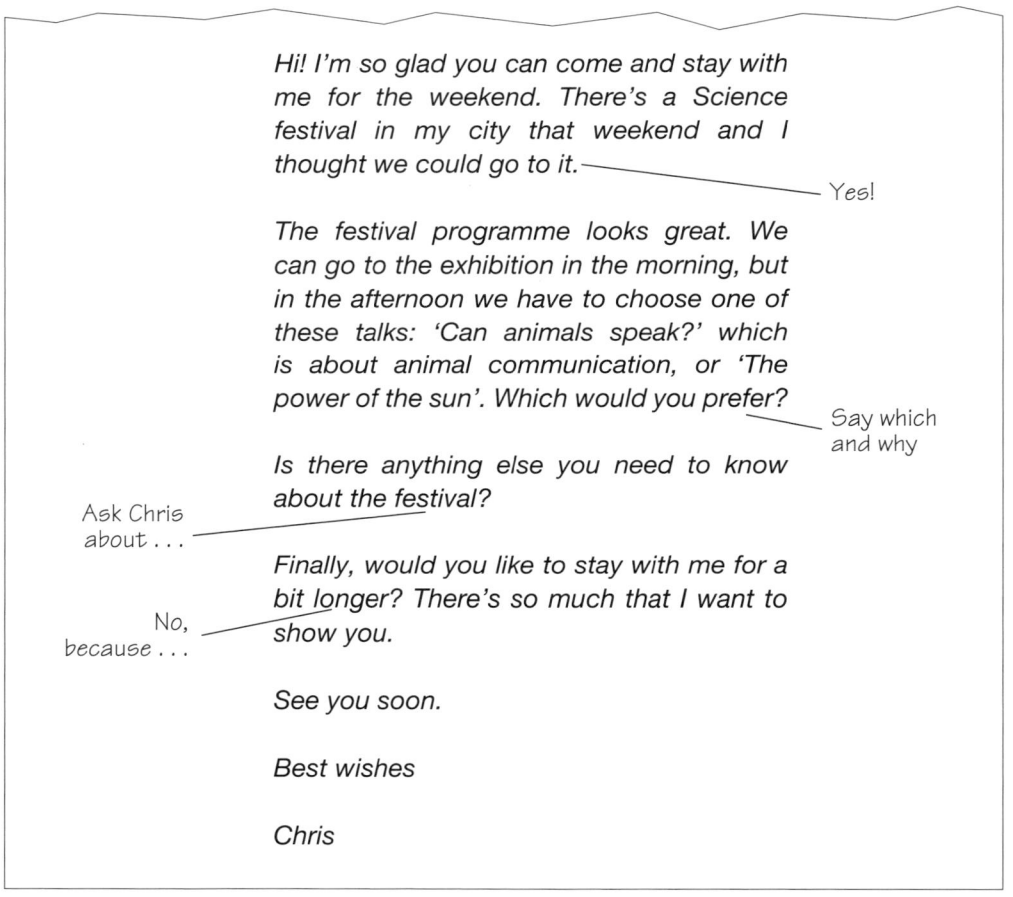

> Hi! I'm so glad you can come and stay with me for the weekend. There's a Science festival in my city that weekend and I thought we could go to it. — Yes!
>
> The festival programme looks great. We can go to the exhibition in the morning, but in the afternoon we have to choose one of these talks: 'Can animals speak?' which is about animal communication, or 'The power of the sun'. Which would you prefer? — Say which and why
>
> Is there anything else you need to know about the festival? — Ask Chris about . . .
>
> Finally, would you like to stay with me for a bit longer? There's so much that I want to show you. — No, because . . .
>
> See you soon.
>
> Best wishes
>
> Chris

Write your **letter**. You must use grammatically correct sentences with accurate spelling and punctuation in a style appropriate for the situation.

Part 2

Write an answer to **one** of the questions **2–5** in this part. Write your answer in **120–180** words in an appropriate style.

2   You have seen this announcement in an international magazine:

> **Friendship today**
> - How do **you** make friends?
> - Do friends have to agree on everything?
>
> The best articles will be published in next month's magazine.

Write your **article**.

3   Your English teacher has asked you to write a story for the college magazine. The story must **begin** with the following words:

When Stella walked into the house, she was astonished to see a suitcase in the hall.

Write your **story**.

4   You have seen this notice in your college English language magazine:

> **STUDENT FILM CLUB**
>
> Help us to choose films for the club! Have you seen a good thriller recently?
>
> Send us a review of a thriller you enjoyed, explaining why you found it exciting and why you think other people would like it.
>
> We will publish the reviews in the club newsletter.

Write your **review**.

5   Answer **one** of the following two questions based on **one** of the titles below.

(a) *Phantom of the Opera* by Gaston Leroux
Your English teacher has given you this essay for homework:

Who was the Phantom of the Opera and what information is given in the story about his past life?

Write your **essay**.

(b) *Great Expectations* by Charles Dickens
You have seen a notice in an English language magazine asking for articles about strange characters in books.

Write an **article** describing Miss Havisham in *Great Expectations*, explaining why she is so strange.

Test 1

PAPER 3 USE OF ENGLISH (45 minutes)

Part 1

For questions **1–12**, read the text below and decide which answer (**A, B, C** or **D**) best fits each gap. There is an example at the beginning (**0**).

Mark your answers **on the separate answer sheet**.

Example:

0 **A** sign   **B** mark   **C** figure   **D** symbol

0	A	B	C	D
				■

Mount Fuji

For the Japanese, Mount Fuji has long been the ultimate **(0)** ..... of beauty. It is incredibly beautiful when seen from any **(1)** ..... , at all times of day and in any season. But the mountain does not only **(2)** ..... a major part in the landscape – it has also inspired poets and artists for centuries, and has come to be **(3)** ..... with Japan itself. From the top, the sides of the mountain **(4)** ..... away, then flatten out before reaching the ground. Here, at ground **(5)** ..... , the foot of the mountain **(6)** ..... an almost perfect circle.

To the north of Mount Fuji **(7)** ..... the famous 'Five Lakes'. The lakeside area is a sea of colour in spring, when the fruit trees are flowering, and it is also a stunning **(8)** ..... in autumn, when the leaves **(9)** ..... first brilliant red, then many shades of brown. **(10)** ..... , many of the best views of Mount Fuji are from these lakes, whose still waters reflect the mountain's beautifully symmetrical outline like a mirror. Both Mount Fuji and its lakes are volcanic in **(11)** ..... , and that is probably why traditional stories say that Mount Fuji appeared overnight; and, for the same reason, it may one day **(12)** ..... just as suddenly!

1	A	edge	B	angle	C	corner	D	curve
2	A	stay	B	keep	C	make	D	play
3	A	identified	B	named	C	recognised	D	considered
4	A	lean	B	give	C	slope	D	take
5	A	floor	B	level	C	height	D	position
6	A	forms	B	does	C	shapes	D	arranges
7	A	situate	B	locate	C	lie	D	exist
8	A	appearance	B	impression	C	look	D	sight
9	A	move	B	pass	C	alter	D	turn
10	A	Especially	B	Given	C	Indeed	D	Nevertheless
11	A	basis	B	cause	C	origin	D	beginning
12	A	fade	B	vanish	C	withdraw	D	cease

Part 2

For questions **13–24**, read the text below and think of the word which best fits each gap. Use only **one** word in each gap. There is an example at the beginning (**0**).

Write your answers **IN CAPITAL LETTERS on the separate answer sheet**.

Example: | 0 | F | O | R |

A man of many parts

Life on a remote Scottish island is wonderfully peaceful. But **(0)** .... one local, Hamish McAlpine, life is far from relaxing. This is because Hamish has fourteen jobs. **(13)** .... he meets me off the ferry, harbour master Hamish is the one and **(14)** .... person in sight. Luckily, he is also the island's taxi driver, so he takes me to the hotel, **(15)** .... he owns. He can even **(16)** .... found serving behind the counter at the local shop.

It all started not **(17)** .... after Hamish married his wife Donna in 1964. The couple were asked **(18)** .... they would like to run the post office. Then Hamish found himself agreeing to become fire chief, policeman and coastguard. Now, having given 35 years of devoted service, Hamish **(19)** .... about to retire. But who will **(20)** .... over his jobs? Can one person do it all or will the jobs have to be split up?

Apart **(21)** .... their week-long honeymoon on the mainland, the couple have had hardly **(22)** .... holidays. 'Donna and I have worked together every day for the last 35 years. But who knows, once we have lots of time on our hands we **(23)** .... find we can't stand the sight of each **(24)** .... ,' says Hamish, his eyes twinkling mischievously.

Part 3

For questions **25–34**, read the text below. Use the word given in capitals at the end of some of the lines to form a word that fits in the gap **in the same line**. There is an example at the beginning (**0**).

Write your answers **IN CAPITAL LETTERS** on the separate answer sheet.

Example: | 0 | S | T | E | A | D | I | L | Y | | | | | | |

The Warrumbungle National Park

The Warrumbungle National Park is (0) .... increasing in **STEADY**
(25) .... with visitors to Australia. Walking, camping and rock **POPULAR**
climbing are the favourite leisure-time (26) .... in this area, **OCCUPY**
but the landscape and wildlife, which are (27) .... varied, also **EXTRAORDINARY**
attract (28) .... and naturalists throughout the different seasons **PHOTOGRAPH**
of the year. Visitors share the park with hundreds of native animals,
such as kangaroos and koalas.

The wonderful (29) .... in Warrumbungle National Park is **SCENE**
the result of (30) .... volcanic activity over a massive area. This **POWER**
produced the many (31) .... rock formations and numerous lakes **SPECTACLE**
visible today, and also the rich soil which enables the abundant
vegetation to grow and flourish.

Walking tracks in the park are clearly marked, and visitors
are (32) .... to keep to these. Many of the walks can be done **COURAGE**
by children and some are (33) .... for pushchairs and wheelchairs. **SUIT**
A relatively easy, but highly rewarding, walk is the 5-kilometre
trek up to Belougery Split Rock, where visitors may be lucky
enough to see eagles flying overhead. More (34) .... walkers can **ENERGY**
try the more demanding 15-kilometre walk to Camp Pincham.
The view there is unforgettable, but it will take even the fittest
walker four or five hours to get there.

Test 1

Part 4

For questions **35–42**, complete the second sentence so that it has a similar meaning to the first sentence, using the word given. **Do not change the word given**. You must use between **two** and **five** words, including the word given. Here is an example (**0**).

Example:

0   You must do exactly what the manager tells you.

  CARRY

  You must .... instructions exactly.

The gap can be filled by the words 'carry out the manager's', so you write:

Example: | **0** | CARRY OUT THE MANAGER'S |

Write **only** the missing words **IN CAPITAL LETTERS** on the separate answer sheet.

---

35   I can't afford to pay for all the books I need on my income.

  HIGH

  My income is .... to pay for all the books I need.

36   Scientists say the climate didn't use to be so warm.

  THAN

  Scientists say the climate is .... be.

37   Your new car is very similar to my brother's.

  LOT

  There is not .... your new car and my brother's.

38   The match will be played tomorrow unless it rains.

  LONG

  The match will be played tomorrow as .... any rain.

39 I am sorry that I did not go to the cinema with Mark.

WISH

I .... to the cinema with Mark.

40 The party was so successful that most people didn't want to go home.

SUCH

The party was .... that most people didn't want to go home.

41 They missed the appointment because the train was late.

RESULT

As a .... late, they missed the appointment.

42 The court convicted Charles of stealing the diamonds.

FOUND

Charles .... stealing the diamonds.

Test 1

PAPER 4 LISTENING (approximately 40 minutes)

Part 1

You will hear people talking in eight different situations. For questions **1–8**, choose the best answer (**A**, **B** or **C**).

1 You hear a woman talking on the radio about a trip to a rock festival.
   Why was she at the rock festival?

   A to surprise her friends

   B to spend time with her son

   C to keep an eye on her son

2 You overhear a man and a woman talking about the woman's first week in a new job.
   What does she say about it?

   A It was frightening.

   B It was boring.

   C It was tiring.

3 On the radio, you hear a review of a new travel book.
   What is the reviewer's opinion of the book?

   A It is generally rather disappointing.

   B It is a surprisingly detailed account.

   C It relies too heavily on written descriptions.

4 You hear a journalist talking about an athlete called Helen Wright.
   What is the journalist's main point?

   A Helen lacks the will to win.

   B Helen has always shown a natural talent.

   C Helen is beginning to take running more seriously.

Paper 4 Listening

5 You overhear a man and a woman talking about holidays.
How did the woman feel about her holiday on a cruise ship?

    A She regretted that the stops had been so short.

    B She thought the accommodation was inadequate.

    C She found the other passengers uninteresting.

6 You turn on the radio and hear a man talking about modern life.
What point is the man making about life today?

    A People are lucky to be given a number of choices.

    B People need to concentrate on improving their lifestyle.

    C People often find life can get too complicated.

7 You hear a writer talking on the radio.
What is she explaining?

    A why she writes about the past

    B how her style of writing has changed

    C where her inspiration comes from

8 You overhear a conversation between two teachers.
What are they planning?

    A an educational trip

    B a sports event

    C a musical event

Test 1

Part 2

On a travel programme, you will hear a man, Jeremy Clark, reporting from Mapé, a tropical island where people go on holiday. For questions **9–18**, complete the sentences.

Mapé – a tropical island

Jeremy has spent a [____9____] on the holiday island of Mapé, and he'd like to stay longer.

Most tourists arrive at Mapé in what's called a [____10____] which connects it to another island.

On one side of Jeremy's hotel there is the beach; on the other there is a [____11____]

The best thing about Port Mapé is the wonderful [____12____] which is held in the evening.

Jeremy travelled around the island on a [____13____] which he hired.

The northern part of the island has both beautiful [____14____] and frightening roads.

Jeremy was particularly impressed by the [____15____] of the fish he saw from the beach.

In a bay near Jeremy's hotel, it's possible to do windsurfing and [____16____], but not other sports.

Jeremy describes the locally produced hotel food as both [__ and __17__]

Jeremy mentions [____18____] as a type of food unavailable on the island.

Paper 4 Listening

Part 3

You will hear five different people talking about their work in art and design. For questions **19–23**, choose from the list (**A–F**) what each speaker says. Use the letters only once. There is one extra letter which you do not need to use.

A I try to limit the amount of work I take on.

Speaker 1	19

B I want to learn to work more quickly.

Speaker 2	20

C I like to see new artistic ideas develop.

Speaker 3	21

D I like to give individual attention to people.

Speaker 4	22

E I try to be practical as well as artistic.

Speaker 5	23

F I enjoy experimenting with different materials.

Test 1

Part 4

You will hear a radio interview with a woman called Ivana Thomas, whose father wrote natural history articles for newspapers and magazines. For questions **24–30**, choose the best answer (**A**, **B** or **C**).

24 Why was Ivana's father pleased to be asked to write a weekly newspaper column?

    A He was bored with the other work he was doing.

    B He had to support a growing family.

    C He had made the suggestion to the newspaper.

25 Why did Ivana's father find his job in a museum frustrating?

    A He wasn't interested in sea creatures.

    B He wasn't very good at detailed work.

    C He wasn't able to study a range of things.

26 Why did Ivana's father take the family on long bus trips?

    A to teach them about wildlife

    B to get ideas for his articles

    C to look for a new place to live

27 What did Ivana's father encourage his children to do on visits to the countryside?

    A take photographs of rare things they saw

    B take notes about anything interesting they found

    C draw the ordinary creatures they observed

28 Why did Ivana and her brothers choose to do similar jobs to their father's?

    A They didn't seriously consider other careers.

    B They were persuaded to do so by their father.

    C They weren't good enough at other subjects to pursue careers in them.

Paper 4 Listening

29 What was different about the articles Ivana's father wrote in his later years?

   A He wrote fewer of them than before.

   B He rewrote some of his previous articles.

   C He responded to his readers' questions.

30 What does Ivana particularly remember about her father?

   A his sense of curiosity

   B the interesting talks he gave

   C how ambitious he was

Test 1

Paper 5 SPEAKING (14 minutes)

You take the Speaking test with another candidate (possibly two candidates), referred to here as your partner. There are two examiners. One will speak to you and your partner and the other will be listening. Both examiners will award marks.

Part 1 (3 minutes)

The examiner asks you and your partner questions about yourselves. You may be asked about things like 'your home town', 'your interests', 'your career plans', etc.

Part 2 (a one-minute 'long turn' for each candidate, plus 20-second response from the second candidate)

The examiner gives you two photographs and asks you to talk about them for one minute. The examiner then asks your partner a question about your photographs and your partner responds briefly.

Then the examiner gives your partner two different photographs. Your partner talks about these photographs for one minute. This time the examiner asks you a question about your partner's photographs and you respond briefly.

Part 3 (approximately 3 minutes)

The examiner asks you and your partner to talk together. You may be asked to solve a problem or try to come to a decision about something. For example, you might be asked to decide the best way to use some rooms in a language school. The examiner gives you a picture to help you but does not join in the conversation.

Part 4 (approximately 4 minutes)

The examiner asks some further questions, which leads to a more general discussion of what you have talked about in Part 3. You may comment on your partner's answers if you wish.

Test 2

Test 2

PAPER 1   READING (1 hour)

Part 1

You are going to read an extract from a novel. For questions **1–8**, choose the answer (**A**, **B**, **C** or **D**) which you think fits best according to the text.

Mark your answers **on the separate answer sheet**.

'He'll be in soon for this,' thought Mrs Bland, who ran the village shop, putting on her glasses to examine the envelope more closely. Every Friday, for over a year, she'd received a letter addressed to Mr Smith. She hadn't, at first, objected when he asked if his post might be sent care of her address. After all, he was new to the village and she liked to oblige people, especially a customer. He'd taken a cottage, he'd explained, a couple of kilometres out of the village and wanted to be sure of getting his letters regularly. So she'd agreed. There seemed no harm in it.

He hadn't been so odd, either, in those first few weeks; a bit untidy, admittedly, and apparently rather shy, but anyone could tell he came from a good background; he was well spoken and polite. There had been gossip about him among the locals, of course. Where had he come from and why had he chosen to live in Stokes Cottage? It had been empty for two years because nobody wanted to live up that lane, far from the main road. The villagers came to the conclusion that the newcomer was from London and had been ill or, more likely, unlucky in love. He had the withdrawn, faded look of illness or disappointment.

As the months passed, however, Mrs Bland became less sure of her decision. With time, he became even less talkative. He would stand silently in the shop, looking out of the window, running his hands through his increasingly long and untidy-looking beard, if another customer was being served. Nobody could draw him into conversation, let alone find out anything about him, and in the end people gave up trying. Some of them complained that he made them feel uneasy and avoided coming into the shop while he was there. But, as Mrs Bland said to them, what could she do? He only came in once a week, on a Friday morning, and she couldn't refuse to serve him on the grounds that he wasn't sociable. 'Besides,' she added to herself, 'I can't start turning people away for no reason.'

She wondered about him, though, and every week looked at the envelope, hoping to find out something. She'd decided that it must contain money, although she couldn't be sure because it was never opened in her presence and even her most inquisitive customers hadn't dared to question him about it. There was clearly something thin and flat inside anyway. The London postmark never varied, and the typewritten address gave no clue as to the sender.

line 27   A storm had broken that Friday morning. Mrs Bland had run to put down newspapers to save the flooring tiles from the worst of the wet and mud, and that's when she saw him coming. He was trudging along with his head bent against the downpour. When Smith entered the shop, Mrs Bland felt the need to begin a conversation immediately, although she knew he would not respond.

'Good morning, Mr Smith. What dreadful weather we're having. Your letter's come.'

'Yes,' said Smith. He took the envelope and put it, without looking at it, into his inside pocket, handing her in exchange the shopping list he always had prepared.

line 33   She read through the list of items, saying each one aloud as she fetched it from the shelf and entered the price in the till. She liked talking. Even when alone, she chatted to herself in her head, but she was afraid of serious conversations. She left that sort of thing to her husband, who was clever with words and sometimes alarmed her with the force of his opinions. You had to be so careful what you said to people in a shop. She would have hated to cause offence, so she limited herself to pleasant chat that said little and harmed nobody. And when Smith was in the shop, she didn't notice his silence so much if she talked, but her thoughts ran alongside her speech, deeper and less comfortable.

30

1   How did Mrs Bland react when Mr Smith first asked her to keep his letters?

   A   She felt sorry for him.
   B   She was curious about him.
   C   She didn't mind helping.
   D   She wasn't sure what to do.

2   In the second paragraph, we learn that the local people were

   A   amused by Mr Smith's shyness.
   B   convinced of Mr Smith's unhappiness.
   C   impressed by Mr Smith's physical appearance.
   D   worried by Mr Smith's odd behaviour.

3   Why did Mrs Bland's attitude to Mr Smith begin to change?

   A   He appeared at the shop at increasingly inconvenient times.
   B   He answered her questions impolitely.
   C   His appearance alarmed some customers.
   D   He no longer made any effort to communicate.

4   How did Mrs Bland respond to people who talked about Mr Smith?

   A   She agreed with their point of view.
   B   She apologised for his behaviour.
   C   She pointed out his right to shop there.
   D   She explained that he was a valuable customer.

5   What gave Mrs Bland the idea that the letters might contain money?

   A   the fact that the sender's name was not shown
   B   the way the envelopes looked
   C   the fact that they came so regularly
   D   the secretive way in which Mr Smith handled them

6   What does the word 'trudging' (line 27) tell us about Mr Smith?

   A   how he was moving
   B   his facial expression
   C   how he was dressed
   D   his physical size

7   What does 'it' (line 33) refer to?

   A   the list
   B   the weekly letter
   C   a price
   D   a product

8   What do we learn about Mrs Bland in the final paragraph?

   A   She found her work unsatisfying.
   B   She was frightened of her husband.
   C   She worried about upsetting her customers.
   D   She found it hard to understand people.

Part 2

You are going to read a newspaper article about an elephant. Seven sentences have been removed from the article. Choose from the sentences **A–H** the one which fits each gap (**9–15**). There is one extra sentence which you do not need to use.

Mark your answers **on the separate answer sheet**.

Saving an elephant

Douglas Turner tells the story of a baby elephant who was taken on a 1,500 km journey in order to save her life.

The first time I saw Wiwin, she looked like a wizened old woman with wrinkly skin, but she was in fact a baby elephant. She had been left behind when her family group was chased back into the forest after being caught raiding a rice field in Southern Sumatra, Indonesia. She had been rescued by the local people, who quickly realised that they lacked the means to care for her.

So she was brought to the local office of the Wildlife Conservation Society. Wiwin was desperate for affection. **9** Because her growing teeth were sore, she had also taken to chewing on anything and everything.

Everyone at the Conservation office was impressed by her spirit; she was clearly a survivor, but having her there presented a number of problems. **10** So the staff desperately contacted anyone who could give advice and began constructing feeding equipment from a length of tubing attached to a plastic bottle. Once they discovered the formula of a blend of cow's milk, coconut water and milk powder, Wiwin started to take in liquids.

There could be no question of releasing her back into the wild. The only option was for her to go to an elephant training centre (ETC), which cared for orphaned elephants. The nearest ETC was 1,500 km away, but transporting Wiwin over that distance would be extremely difficult, especially as she was so weak. **11** We set off in convoy. Wiwin was in a jeep on a cushion of coconut palms, with the wildlife centre staff; I followed with a photographer.

The first twenty-four hours went well. **12** Mostly, we travelled in the cool of the night, driving through sleeping villages and setting up camp at daybreak, putting up a tent to give Wiwin shade.

We continued on our way in the late afternoon and drove straight into a torrential rainstorm. Trees were blown down, even blocking the road in places. **13** We stopped for breakfast at a roadside café, where one local peered in and touched her nervously as if expecting an electric shock.

After three days we arrived at the Sebanga ETC, to be met by the resident vet, Joanne Hammatt. She agreed that we should try to see if the elephant with the newborn calf might let Wiwin into their group to feed. **14** However, she did soon settle into life at Sebanga, interacting well with the other elephants.

So, after a week we left Wiwin at the centre. Regular updates from Joanne kept us informed of Wiwin's improving condition. It could be questioned whether we were justified in putting all this effort into keeping just one animal alive – in order for it to live a limited life in captivity. **15** She was a symbol of hope for a group of weary conservationists who are very aware that it takes an enormous amount of time and stamina to make a difference.

A Despite all this, Wiwin managed to sleep contentedly.

B However, as we were told they had an elephant with a newborn calf, which might provide a suitable foster mother for Wiwin, it seemed too good an opportunity to miss.

C But Wiwin was more than just an orphan elephant.

D Even when she was sleepy, she would wrap her trunk around the nearest person, pleading for company.

E After weighing her, our fears were confirmed.

F Introductions were made the next day, but Wiwin could not be separated from her bottle, so unfortunately we had to give up the fostering idea.

G Wiwin determined our schedule: if she was tired we stopped, and if she was hungry we opened a coconut and fed her.

H The most immediate of these was her unwillingness to drink anything in the sweltering heat.

Test 2

Part 3

You are going to read a magazine article about students who have travelled the world before going to university. For questions **16–30**, choose from the students (**A–E**). The students may be chosen more than once. When more than one answer is required, these may be given in any order.

Mark your answers **on the separate answer sheet**.

Which student(s)

need not have worried about health problems?	16
says he wanted to be more adventurous than his friends?	17
had to delay the start of his trip?	18
was concerned about an aspect of his preparations for the trip?	19
gained unexpected benefits from a limited budget?	20
changed his original plans in order to explore another place?	21
found different ways of earning money while he was away from home?	22
was unaccustomed to travelling alone?	23
wanted to avoid having a fixed programme?	24
changed his study plans as a result of his experiences abroad?	25
found accommodation through some colleagues?	26
was forced to alter his route?	27
were aware of personal security when travelling?	28 29
disliked the restrictions of a limited budget?	30

34

Taking off

Five young people remember their 'gap year' experiences, when they travelled the world between finishing school and going to university.

A Tom Baker

After my exams, I read through all the gap year literature, but I'd had enough of having to turn up to lessons every day at school. So I flew to New Zealand, without any structured plans, just to see what happened. I had to live very cheaply, so I didn't use public transport, preferring to hitch-hike the long distances between the towns. I was amazed how generous people were. I was always being picked up by strangers and invited into their homes after nothing more than a conversation at the roadside. My hosts invited me to climb volcanoes, go trekking with them, even play a part in a short film. In a way, I learned just as much about life as I did when I was at university back in the UK.

B Robin Talbot

It all began when I was on summer holiday staying at a friend's house in New York. By the autumn, I was convinced I didn't want to leave and I stayed there for a year. I worked three days a week in a bar and two nights in a restaurant, which gave me plenty to live on. The Brazilian band that worked in the bar offered me a room in their apartment, and we played salsa music and had barbecues all summer. I realised eventually that I couldn't be a waiter for ever, so I came back to university.

C Mark Irvin

I couldn't face another three years studying straight after school so, like many of my classmates, I decided to do a round-the-world trip. I wanted to set off at the end of the summer, but it took six months of working before I had enough money. I'd planned my route so that I'd be travelling with friends for part of the way and alone the rest of the time. In Japan I met some incredibly generous people who invited me into their homes. I found their culture fascinating. But in Australia it was less interesting because it was more difficult to meet the locals, as I could only afford to stay in hostels and these were full of British travellers like me.

D Simon Barton

Going to Latin America was quite a courageous decision for me, and the first time I had travelled without a fixed route or any companions. I was worried that my last-minute Spanish course would not be enough. I was originally planning to fly to Mexico, then go overland by bus to Belize, but a hurricane intervened and it was too risky. So I went west by bus to Guatemala. The people were very friendly, but as I'm blond-haired and blue-eyed they stared a bit, which didn't bother me. I just smiled. I dutifully kept all my important stuff on me, as suggested in the *World Travellers' Guidebook*, but I didn't run into any trouble at all. And despite what I thought might happen, I ate anything and everything and didn't have any problems. It was great! I'm already saving for my next trip.

E Andrew West

Everyone I knew was going to Australia, but I wanted to go somewhere more exotic, less predictable. I went with 'Quest Overseas', who arrange gap-year holidays. I started in Ecuador with a three-week Spanish course, then went off trekking in the Andes, which was tough. It's a good thing I had my first-aid kit, I was covered in scratches! I had arranged my flight back, but I put it off to go touring in Mexico for two weeks with some friends I'd made. My advice would be, plan ahead, but don't worry if things change. Keep your cash in various places in your clothing, and take advice about the places to avoid at night. I never felt scared, I just enjoyed the adventure. And when I came back I decided to do a degree in South American History, which I'd never have considered before. I thought living in a flat again would be dull, but in fact I'd had enough of always being on the move.

Test 2

PAPER 2 WRITING (1 hour 20 minutes)

Part 1

You **must** answer this question. Write your answer in **120–150** words in an appropriate style.

1   You have received an email from your English friend Alex. Read Alex's email and the notes you have made. Then write an email to Alex using **all** your notes.

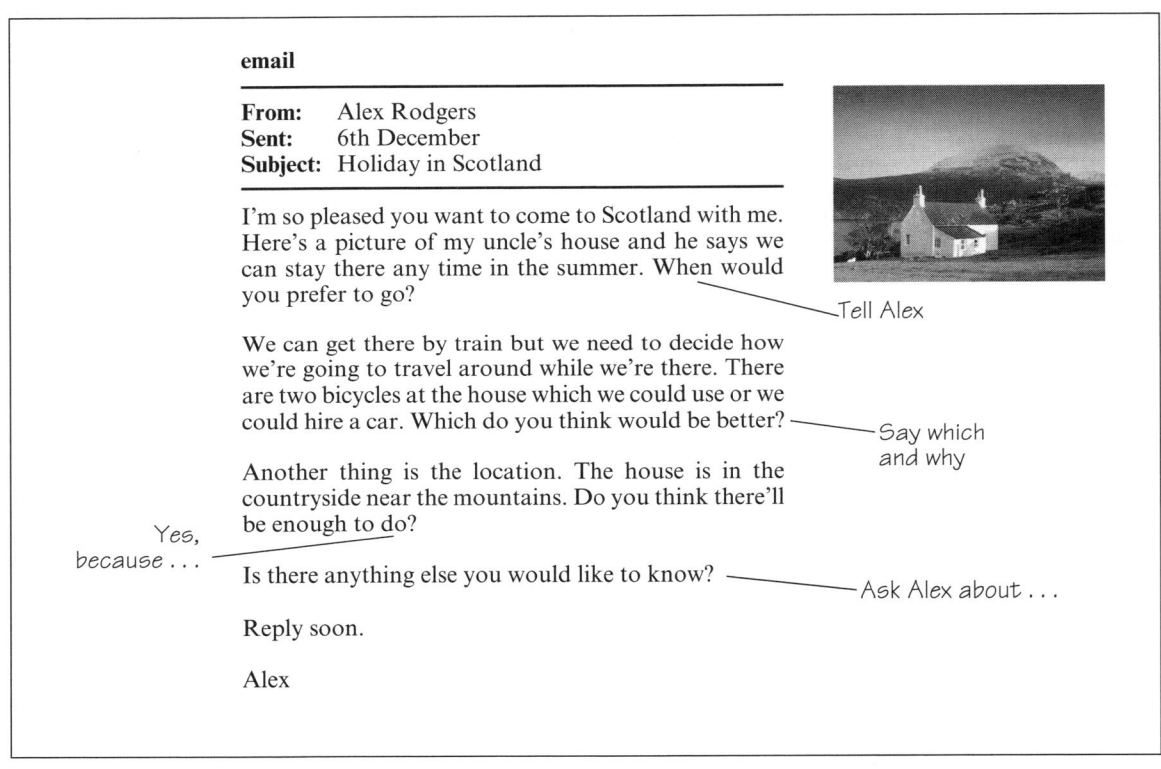

email

From: Alex Rodgers
Sent: 6th December
Subject: Holiday in Scotland

I'm so pleased you want to come to Scotland with me. Here's a picture of my uncle's house and he says we can stay there any time in the summer. When would you prefer to go? ———Tell Alex

We can get there by train but we need to decide how we're going to travel around while we're there. There are two bicycles at the house which we could use or we could hire a car. Which do you think would be better? ——— Say which and why

Another thing is the location. The house is in the countryside near the mountains. Do you think there'll be enough to do? ——— Yes, because ...

Is there anything else you would like to know? ——— Ask Alex about ...

Reply soon.

Alex

Write your **email**. You must use grammatically correct sentences with accurate spelling and punctuation in a style appropriate for the situation.

Part 2

Write an answer to **one** of the questions **2–5** in this part. Write your answer in **120–180** words in an appropriate style.

2   You have seen this announcement in an international magazine:

> **Competition!   Twentieth-century inventions**
>
> Aeroplane   Computer   Television
>
> Which **one** of these three inventions of the 20th century do you think has changed our lives the most? The best article will be published in next month's magazine.

Write your **article**.

3   Your English teacher has asked you to write a story for the college magazine. The story must **begin** with the following words:

Mark opened the envelope, read the letter and immediately started to pack his bag.

Write your **story**.

4   You have seen this advertisement in an international magazine:

> **WANT A SUMMER JOB WITH A DIFFERENCE?**
>
> A British film company working in your country has the following temporary job vacancies:
> - actors for crowd scenes
> - make-up and costume assistants
> - kitchen workers.
>
> Write to Mrs Simmons, saying which job you are interested in and why you would be suitable.

Write your **letter of application**.

5   Answer **one** of the following two questions based on **one** of the titles below.

(a) *Phantom of the Opera* by Gaston Leroux
   This is part of a letter from your English-speaking friend Clare:

> *I've finished reading 'Phantom of the Opera' now. At the end, I felt sorry for Erik. How did you feel about him? Write and tell me. Clare*

   Write your **letter**.

(b) *Great Expectations* by Charles Dickens
   Your English teacher has given you this essay for homework:

   What are Pip's 'Great Expectations'? Give your opinion on whether he has what he expected by the end of the book.

   Write your **essay**.

Test 2

PAPER 3   USE OF ENGLISH (45 minutes)

Part 1

For questions **1–12**, read the text below and decide which answer (**A, B, C** or **D**) best fits each gap. There is an example at the beginning (**0**).

Mark your answers **on the separate answer sheet**.

Example:

0   **A** basis   **B** foundation   **C** source   **D** reason

| 0 | A | B | **C** | D |

Proof that silence is golden for studying

The combination of music and study has long been a **(0)** ..... of disagreement between adults and children. Parents and teachers alike maintain that silence is important when learning, **(1)** ..... youngsters insist that their favourite sounds help them concentrate.

Now a study shows that the grown-ups have been **(2)** ..... all along. Psychologists in Florida tested how fast students wrote essays with and without music in the **(3)** .... They found that the sounds **(4)** ..... progress down by about sixty words per hour. 'This demonstrates clearly that it is difficult to **(5)** ..... with listening and writing at the same time,' said Dr Sarah Randall. She also **(6)** ..... to the conclusion that it is a myth that instrumental music is less distracting than vocals. 'All types of music **(7)** ..... the same effect,' she said in her report. 'One's ability to pay attention and write fluently is likely to be **(8)** ..... by both vocal and instrumental music,' she added.

Dr Randall claimed the research **(9)** ..... that the idea that music could improve performance was wrong. 'Writing an essay is a complex **(10)** .... You are recalling information and putting it in **(11)** .... An additional stimulus in the form of music is bound to distract. But music is not the only distractor. What is **(12)** ..... worrying is that more and more teenagers are studying in front of the television.'

38

1	**A**	whereas	**B**	unlike	**C**	besides	**D**	despite
2	**A**	precise	**B**	right	**C**	valid	**D**	true
3	**A**	setting	**B**	background	**C**	surrounding	**D**	circumstances
4	**A**	slowed	**B**	reduced	**C**	lowered	**D**	decreased
5	**A**	manage	**B**	support	**C**	cope	**D**	stand
6	**A**	reached	**B**	drew	**C**	arrived	**D**	came
7	**A**	made	**B**	had	**C**	brought	**D**	kept
8	**A**	disturbed	**B**	interfered	**C**	bothered	**D**	shocked
9	**A**	pointed	**B**	displayed	**C**	demonstrated	**D**	presented
10	**A**	project	**B**	concern	**C**	scheme	**D**	task
11	**A**	order	**B**	arrangement	**C**	line	**D**	pattern
12	**A**	partly	**B**	largely	**C**	particularly	**D**	mainly

Test 2

Part 2

For questions **13–24**, read the text below and think of the word which best fits each gap. Use only **one** word in each gap. There is an example at the beginning (**0**).

Write your answers **IN CAPITAL LETTERS** on the separate answer sheet.

Example: | 0 | O | F |

A model village

In 1861, George Cadbury took over control **(0)** .... his father's chocolate factory in Birmingham, England. At that time, it was hard **(13)** .... ordinary working people to find comfortable houses in **(14)** .... they could afford to live, and Cadbury wanted to improve the situation. He started by moving his chocolate factory into the countryside. He thought that **(15)** .... each of his workers had his own house in a healthy environment then this would result **(16)** .... a happy family life.

The first 143 houses of his model village, called Bournville, **(17)** .... built on ground next to the factory in 1895. A **(18)** .... workers were able to buy theirs cheaply while the majority paid a fair rent. **(19)** .... house had a large garden. All these gardens were cultivated to supply the villagers **(20)** .... fresh fruit and vegetables. **(21)** .... tenth of the village area was given over to public spaces **(22)** .... that there was somewhere for residents to socialise and where community projects could **(23)** .... place.

Bournville is a continuing success story and today has more than 8,000 homes. Cadbury's model village gave rise **(24)** .... the idea of the 'garden city' and has had many imitators in Europe and the United States.

Part 3

For questions **25–34**, read the text below. Use the word given in capitals at the end of some of the lines to form a word that fits in the gap **in the same line**. There is an example at the beginning (**0**).

Write your answers **IN CAPITAL LETTERS on the separate answer sheet**.

Example: | 0 | C | E | N | T | R | A | L | | | | | | | |

City centre traffic problems

The amount of traffic in the crowded (**0**) .... districts of some **CENTRE**
of our largest cities is a major problem these days. Over the years,
(**25**) .... schemes of traffic management have been tried, none **VARY**
of which can be said to have been entirely (**26**) .... In order to **SUCCESS**
(**27**) .... people to leave their cars at home, especially on shorter trips, it **COURAGE**
is becoming increasingly common for cities to impose a fee on those drivers
who choose to come into the city centre.

Some schemes take advantage of the latest technology – for example, in one
city (**28**) .... is made by a card on the car's windscreen which is scanned **PAY**
(**29**) .... This is meant to speed up the flow of traffic, but the scheme has **AUTOMATIC**
a major (**30**) .... as the amount that drivers have to pay changes during the **ADVANTAGE**
day and, as a result, it is not (**31**) .... for long queues to build up just before **USUAL**
a cheaper charging period comes into (**32**) .... However, the system is **OPERATE**
gradually gaining in (**33**) .... with motorists, although it has to be admitted it **POPULAR**
may not provide a total (**34**) .... to the problem of traffic congestion. **SOLVE**

Test 2

Part 4

For questions **35–42**, complete the second sentence so that it has a similar meaning to the first sentence, using the word given. **Do not change the word given.** You must use between **two** and **five** words, including the word given. Here is an example (**0**).

Example:

0   You must do exactly what the manager tells you.

   CARRY

   You must .... instructions exactly.

The gap can be filled by the words 'carry out the manager's', so you write:

Example: | **0** | *CARRY OUT THE MANAGER'S* |

Write **only** the missing words **IN CAPITAL LETTERS** on the separate answer sheet.

---

35   'I can't understand German as well as I used to,' said Lucy.

   BETTER

   'I used to understand .... do now,' said Lucy.

36   Sometimes tiredness causes the machine operators to make mistakes.

   BECAUSE

   Sometimes mistakes .... the tiredness of the machine operators.

37   No one has ever stolen my car.

   HAD

   I have .... stolen.

38   My parents met for the first time thirty years ago.

   THAT

   It .... my parents first met.

39 There are fewer people in the gym class than there were last week.

AS

There .... people in the gym class as there were last week.

40 Kevin started playing golf when he was twelve.

TOOK

Kevin .... the age of twelve.

41 'It was Pierre who left the door unlocked!' said Mary.

ACCUSED

Mary .... the door unlocked.

42 We walked through the jungle until we could go no further.

FAR

We walked .... go through the jungle.

Test 2

PAPER 4 LISTENING (approximately 40 minutes)

Part 1

You will hear people talking in eight different situations. For questions **1–8**, choose the best answer (**A**, **B** or **C**).

1   You hear a student talking about a school magazine he publishes.
    What does he need at the moment?

    A more help

    B more articles

    C more funds

2   You hear a British woman talking about naming children.
    What is her opinion on naming children?

    A She likes to avoid the most common names.

    B She thinks names will become more and more strange.

    C She is in favour of creating completely new names.

3   You hear a man being interviewed on the radio.
    What is his current occupation?

    A a reporter

    B a critic

    C an author

4   You hear an athlete talking about some Olympic trials he took part in.
    How does he feel about his performance?

    A He realises that he did not concentrate enough.

    B He accepts that he had no chance against top athletes.

    C He regrets that he was not in better physical condition.

5   You overhear two friends talking about music.
    How did the man first find out about his new CD?

    A   He read about it.

    B   He heard part of it.

    C   He was told about it.

6   You overhear a man talking about the competitions that he and his wife enter.
    What did his favourite prize allow him to do?

    A   go on an interesting flight

    B   stay in a luxurious place

    C   own a prestigious car

7   You hear a woman talking about her job, which involves inspecting mountain paths.
    What aspect of the job does she sometimes find annoying?

    A   the work schedule

    B   the weather

    C   the walkers

8   On a radio programme, you hear a mother talking about her relationship with her daughter.
    What is she surprised about?

    A   her daughter's decision to leave home

    B   how her daughter has been able to help her

    C   the way that her daughter's attitude has changed

Part 2

You will hear an interview with Alan Burgess, who has just returned from the Arctic where he was filming polar bears. For questions **9–18**, complete the sentences.

Filming polar bears

It took the team approximately [_____ **9**] to make the film.

Of all the places Alan went to, [_____ **10**] was the coldest.

Alan found that clothes made of [_____ **11**] were best for keeping warm.

The team disguised their camera equipment with [_____ **12**] paint.

Polar bears have a strong [_____ **13**].

In the summer, polar bears may lose as much as [_____ **14**] of their body weight.

Polar bears eat plants in order to obtain [_____ **15**] to improve their usual diet.

Baby polar bears can be seen playing in the snow from the month of [_____ **16**].

On one occasion, a polar bear almost managed to enter Alan's [_____ **17**].

Alan is going to work on a number of [_____ **18**] for university students.

Part 3

You will hear five different people talking about their experiences as owners of small local shops. For questions **19–23**, choose from the list (**A–F**) what each speaker says. Use the letters only once. There is one extra letter which you do not need to use.

A I think customers are starting to value small shops more.

　　　　　　　　　　　　　　　　　　　　　　　Speaker 1　[　] 19

B I don't mind hard work as long as I can be my own boss.

　　　　　　　　　　　　　　　　　　　　　　　Speaker 2　[　] 20

C I think small shop owners should lower their prices to compete.

　　　　　　　　　　　　　　　　　　　　　　　Speaker 3　[　] 21

D I am satisfied with my relationship with shops nearby.

　　　　　　　　　　　　　　　　　　　　　　　Speaker 4　[　] 22

E I feel competition may one day force me to close down.

　　　　　　　　　　　　　　　　　　　　　　　Speaker 5　[　] 23

F I provide a service which older people find very important.

Test 2

Part 4

You will hear an interview with the television actress Donna Denton. For questions **24–30**, choose the best answer (**A**, **B** or **C**).

24 As a child, Donna started going to dancing classes because

   A her mother persuaded her to.

   B they were relatively inexpensive.

   C she wanted to be with friends.

25 What did Donna feel when she first went to dancing classes?

   A disappointed by the attitude of the teacher

   B unconcerned about her position in the class

   C embarrassed because she was not a good dancer

26 What did Donna do to get a place at Knightswell Stage School?

   A She took part in a musical show.

   B She got her parents to pay in advance.

   C She gave a demonstration of her skills.

27 At stage school, Donna initially had problems because of

   A the behaviour of other pupils at the school.

   B the amount of time she spent travelling.

   C the need to follow a particular school rule.

28 Donna believes that she won the school singing competition because

   A she had learnt to be less nervous when performing.

   B she had chosen to perform her favourite song.

   C she had been practising one particular song for years.

29 What does Donna say about her first parts on television?

    A A private teacher helped her find them.

    B They were useful in developing her career.

    C It was easy enough for students to get them.

30 When talking about the near future, Donna says that

    A she has agreed to record a music CD soon.

    B she has accepted an unexpected invitation.

    C she has had to make a difficult choice.

Test 2

Paper 5 SPEAKING (14 minutes)

You take the Speaking test with another candidate (possibly two candidates), referred to here as your partner. There are two examiners. One will speak to you and your partner and the other will be listening. Both examiners will award marks.

Part 1 (3 minutes)

The examiner asks you and your partner questions about yourselves. You may be asked about things like 'your home town', 'your interests', 'your career plans', etc.

Part 2 (a one-minute 'long turn' for each candidate, plus 20-second response from the second candidate)

The examiner gives you two photographs and asks you to talk about them for one minute. The examiner then asks your partner a question about your photographs and your partner responds briefly.

Then the examiner gives your partner two different photographs. Your partner talks about these photographs for one minute. This time the examiner asks you a question about your partner's photographs and you respond briefly.

Part 3 (approximately 3 minutes)

The examiner asks you and your partner to talk together. You may be asked to solve a problem or try to come to a decision about something. For example, you might be asked to decide the best way to use some rooms in a language school. The examiner gives you a picture to help you but does not join in the conversation.

Part 4 (approximately 4 minutes)

The examiner asks some further questions, which leads to a more general discussion of what you have talked about in Part 3. You may comment on your partner's answers if you wish.

Test 3

Test 3

PAPER 1 READING (1 hour)

Part 1

You are going to read an extract from a novel about a little girl called Pixie. For questions **1–8**, choose the answer (**A**, **B**, **C** or **D**) which you think fits best according to the text.

Mark your answers **on the separate answer sheet**.

Her father had been a big handsome man with a fine head of hair, a paintbrush in his hand, paint threading along the canvas making a bird look like an angel. He was the famous James Harley Savage, son of Harley Talbot Savage, brother of Norman Backhouse Savage. It was an illustrious family.

From when she was old enough to hold a pencil, the little girl Pixie Harley Savage had been taught about vanishing points in pictures, and was made to work out at the start where the horizon was going to be, and how to make things at the front bigger than things at the back. No matter how young, she had never been allowed to scribble with a pencil or crayon. Nor had she been allowed to do stick people like every other child, or square houses with symmetrical windows and a carefully curving path to the front door with a round tree on one side.

line 9 It was unacceptable to do drawings like that.

Her father's hands skimmed across the paper and out of the end of his pencil came a bird, a twig for it to perch on, behind it a branch. 'See?' he said. 'Like that.'

It was a gifted family, but it seemed that the gift had passed Pixie by. Even after so many patient lessons, from the end of her pencil came only hard ugly lines, and a bird that looked like a surprised fish.

She was ashamed of her own big muscly legs and her round face. But the shame of showing this ugly bird to her father and the rest of her family was unendurable.

She heard the silence and saw the ring of shocked faces among her family.

'Oh, but you are very artistic and terribly creative,' her mother said quickly, with something like fear in her voice.

There was a moment's silence.

'In your own way, of course.'

Someone cleared their throat.

'And you never know, these things blossom later on sometimes.'

At school they had known she was a Savage, and hoped for wonders. Her teacher, Miss McGovern, was even willing to see them when there were none. It had taken a long time, but finally she had come to expect no more wonders.

'Use your imaginations, girls,' Miss McGovern would say, but what Pixie drew was never what she meant by *imagination*. Pixie was interested in the veins of the leaf, how photosynthesis worked and why they turned brown or orange in the autumn.

'You make a plant look like a machine,' Miss McGovern accused.

Pixie's sister, Celeste, had always been a proper Savage. Celeste had known about things at the back of a picture being smaller than things at the front without ever having to be told. She had a way of being dreamy, slightly untidy but lovely, even in her old pink pyjamas, thinking interesting thoughts behind her lovely green

line 33 eyes. Celeste's birds made Father laugh with surprise and pleasure in a way Pixie's never did. Celeste had a knack for other things, too; she was always catching Pixie in moments when she would rather have been alone. Celeste's reflection would join Pixie's frowning into the mirror. 'That lipstick, Pix,' she would say in her sophisticated way, 'it makes you look like a clown.' She was not the older sister, but acted as though she was, not showing Pixie the respect she might have received from a less critical younger sister.

'Why did you call me Pixie?' she asked her mother once, when puberty was making her look into mirrors. 'You were such a beautiful baby,' her mother said, and smiled into the air at the memory of that beautiful baby, not at the face of her plain daughter.

Pixie decided she looked interesting. But later she realised she was simply ordinary: ordinary brown eyes, ordinary brown hair. An ordinary small nose, an ordinary mouth. No one would ever find her fascinating across a crowded room. 'So like your grandmother,' her mother had sighed.

As a child, she could not do much, but she could refuse to answer to the name of the beautiful baby who had turned into herself. 'Harley,' she insisted. 'My name is Harley.'

Paper 1 Reading

1 When Pixie was young, her parents thought that she should
  A get pleasure out of being creative.
  B try not to copy other people's drawings.
  C be shown how to draw properly.
  D be allowed to use her own imagination.

2 In line 9, 'that' refers to drawings which
  A were lacking in originality.
  B were very similar to each other.
  C were done with a pencil or crayon.
  D were of everyday objects.

3 When Pixie drew the bird,
  A she didn't need to put much effort into it.
  B she was trying to please her father.
  C she didn't care what it looked like.
  D she was determined to make it look unusual.

4 What did Pixie's family think of her artistic ability?
  A They were convinced that she would be a good artist one day.
  B They didn't agree on whether she was artistic or not.
  C They found it hard to admit that she had no talent.
  D They were sorry she wouldn't listen to their opinions.

5 What was Miss McGovern's attitude towards Pixie?
  A She was pleased Pixie was showing an interest in science.
  B She continued to hope that Pixie would display her family's creativity.
  C She realised that Pixie was using her imagination in a different way.
  D She tried at first to convince herself that Pixie was typical of her family.

6 What does 'knack' mean in line 33?
  A an ability to do something
  B an ambition to be the best
  C a desire to be noticed
  D a need to be certain about something

7 What do we find out about Celeste?
  A She tried to help Pixie.
  B She worked hard to understand things.
  C She took trouble with her looks.
  D She looked down on Pixie.

8 Pixie decided to be called Harley because she
  A wanted to make her mother annoyed.
  B knew she had not turned out as expected.
  C felt a need to change her appearance.
  D wanted to be more like her father.

53

Part 2

You are going to read an article about two brothers who have become successful businessmen in the UK. Seven sentences have been removed from the article. Choose from the sentences **A–H** the one which fits each gap (**9–15**). There is one extra sentence which you do not need to use.

Mark your answers **on the separate answer sheet**.

From £5 to £250 million

He came to Britain as a 16-year-old with a handful of qualifications, £5 in his pocket and a burning ambition to leave his childhood in Kenya behind him. Vijay Patel was brought up in one room with his brother, Bhikhu, as his schoolteacher mother struggled to raise her family after her husband died. Thirty-five years later, Vijay, 51, and his brother own a pharmaceutical company which employs more than 600 people and does £200 million worth of business each year. Together they are worth £254 million – and now they have been jointly named 'Entrepreneur of the Year'.

It is an inspirational tale. **9** He says: 'We are very pleased and very surprised to have been given this kind of recognition. It has really been about a will to succeed and a determination to distance ourselves from the difficulties of our early life.' He also praises his mother. 'She is an incredible lady. She taught us hard work, honesty and punctuality and we have based our lives on those qualities.'

Vijay's father was a timber merchant who lived with his wife in the village of Eidoret, 200 miles north of Nairobi, and died when Vijay was six. At the age of 16, Vijay and his brother, who was two years older, kissed their mother goodbye and promised to bring her to Britain when they made their fortunes. 'It was 1967 and I had little more than my qualifications and a few pounds in my pocket,' says Vijay. **10** And so he set about trying to achieve just that.

Typically, Vijay looks on the bright side. 'When you start from zero, things can't get any worse.' **11** The pair of them certainly had that.

'My brother and I were determined to better ourselves and Britain was the land of opportunity,' he says.

Vijay enrolled at a college in north London, and did courses in physics, chemistry and biology, washing dishes in a restaurant at night to earn his keep. He gained a degree at the College of Pharmacy in Leicester. After graduating, he opened a chemist's shop in 1975 – he was 24. He made it his business to know all his customers' names, their children and what conditions they suffered from. **12**

By 1982, he owned six shops and sales had doubled. From there it was a short step from buying medicines for his own shops (he now has 21) to supplying other pharmacies, then hospitals and wholesalers. **13**

Brother Bhikhu, an architect by training, joined Vijay in 1982 to add some 'financial discipline' to the company. Vijay says: 'My brother and I have built this business together. I simply couldn't have done it without him. We know each other inside out.' **14**

Vijay is keen to continue putting something back into the country he has made his own. 'We hope we are model citizens and would like to remain so,' he says. 'My brother and I have enormous ambition and drive, but we were also lucky enough to live in a country that never stood in our way,' he says. **15** His message for young people is to do the same: 'Identify your aim, and do not let anything deter you from achieving that goal.'

54

A 'But to go with those, I had a tremendous ambition to make something of myself,' he recalls.

B As he puts it, 'If you cannot trust your family, then who can you trust?'

C Instead, he hopes that his sons will take over the business after they finish their studies.

D 'We took every opportunity it gave us.'

E According to him, in those circumstances, 'You have only one way to go, and that's up – if there is a hunger in your belly for success.'

F Yet despite his wealth and this award, Vijay remains modest about his success.

G 'The idea was that when people had something wrong with them, they went straight to Mr Patel,' he says.

H Last year, company profits hit £13.8 million.

Part 3

You are going to read a newspaper article about four people who have written travel books. For questions **16–30**, choose from the people (**A–D**). The people may be chosen more than once.

Mark your answers **on the separate answer sheet**.

Of which writer is the following stated?

She does not make decisions in advance.	16
She used to be a journalist.	17
She has given up travelling.	18
She writes in an informal way.	19
She travels with the intention of putting her experiences into print.	20
She was undecided about her future when she was young.	21
One of her trips was not a success.	22
Her writing reflects events as they happened.	23
She has written a very successful book.	24

Which writer says

she took no notice of other people's opinions when planning one trip?	25
on one trip, just staying alive took up most of her time?	26
she takes pleasure in her surroundings?	27
she chose her method of transport because of lack of funds?	28
she is confident of finding solutions to problems?	29
she likes to escape from everyday pressures?	30

On the road

A Eleanor Young

Young has written a book about a journey which took seven months. Beginning in Beijing, she headed west out of China and then south to Kashmir. The 20 years of her life until then had been varied – she had been a correspondent for a French weekly, she had sailed in the Olympics and skied internationally, but her main love was travelling. She had made a similar journey in Central Asia and had a minor success with the resulting book. When she writes she thinks of her audience as one family member or one good friend. She writes what was seen and felt, the way it turned up on the road – her descriptions of the camel journey are mixed with discussions about politicians and images of a girl with her hair in a hundred plaits.

B Fiona Dalton

When Dalton visited the bottom tip of Chile and saw the edge of the ice-field, she decided to cross Antarctica. She tried not to be discouraged by others who had done it. 'The men who had skied across alone didn't know how to deal with the idea of someone happy to take a plane some of the way, but I wanted to do the trip my own way.' She spent seven months crossing the continent, pitching tents on the sea ice. Dalton says that as a woman, her reasons for exploration are different from those of men. 'Men have done it to show they can win. I may go to see what the environment can teach me, or to feel the air and see what it looks like. Or just sit around and appreciate the scenery.' She is a writer who explores the world in order to write. She says, 'It also suits me to get away. I love to free myself from the bills and the bank manager. Antarctica is perfect for that.' It was, however, the most testing environment she has ever experienced – it could be 'a full-time job just surviving'.

C Ruth Moore

On her first trip, aged 24, Moore hitch-hiked through Nigeria, canoed down the Congo and rode horseback across Cameroon. What started as a year-long trip turned into a three-and-a-half-year journey. 'The emptiness that lay ahead was wonderful – days waiting to be filled.' She was raised in the African bush and her mother and grandmother had grown up in China. 'I don't know where I belong. My family thought it was totally normal that I had a larger view of the world.' She dismisses fear. 'Wild animals will look for an escape route rather than attack,' she says. Amongst other things, Moore has devised her own cure for homesickness. 'You can always improvise something. I felt homesick for eggs for breakfast while floating down the river, so I had eggs – crocodile eggs – and felt much better.' Moore does believe that a woman's approach is different. She rarely undertakes journeys with an ultimate aim, goal or destination – she decides as she goes along, often with the flip of a coin.

D Sally Wade

Wade is probably more of an ex-explorer – her last journey has put her off. Wade was born in Queensland, Australia. She was sent to boarding school, then just wandered about – studying music, biology and later Japanese. At 25, Wade bought a couple of camels and rode them over 2,000 kilometres across the Australian outback. Her account became a best-seller. 'I never intended to write about it – it was a private thing. I wanted to get to know aboriginal culture and the desert. It was a glorious trip. I went by camel because I was broke and couldn't afford a vehicle.' Then in 1992 she joined a group of Rabari in India. Wade's account of that Indian journey with them tells of failure. 'The two trips were not comparable.' She tried to live a Rabari existence – except that she could always leave. She remained an outsider.

Test 3

PAPER 2 WRITING (1 hour 20 minutes)

Part 1

You **must** answer this question. Write your answer in **120–150** words in an appropriate style.

---

1   You are helping to organise a concert at your college. The local English language newspaper is sending a reporter, Jane Nolan, to the concert. You have received an email from Jane Nolan. Read Mrs Nolan's email and the notes you have made. Then write an email to Mrs Nolan using **all** your notes.

---

email

From: Jane Nolan
Sent: 16th May
Subject: College concert

I am pleased to say that I am able to come to your college concert on 6th July. Our readers are always very interested in events like these. — *Good!*

I would be grateful if you could give me a little more information about the concert. What kind of music will be performed? — *Describe the concert*

I will need to take some photos, so could you tell me when I will have the best opportunity to do this? — *Suggest...*

Also could you let me know who I should interview and why? — *Tell Mrs Nolan who and why*

Yours sincerely,

Jane Nolan

Write your **email**. You must use grammatically correct sentences with accurate spelling and punctuation in a style appropriate for the situation.

Paper 2 Writing

Part 2

Write an answer to **one** of the questions **2–5** in this part. Write your answer in **120–180** words in an appropriate style.

2   Your class wants to go out to a restaurant at the end of the course. Your English teacher has asked you to write a review of a restaurant you like. Include information about the food and the atmosphere and explain why it would be suitable for your class.

   Write your **review**.

3   Your English teacher has asked you to write a story for the college magazine. The story must **begin** with the following words:

   Simon turned on the television and was amazed to see his own face on the screen.

   Write your **story**.

4   You have had a class discussion on how to improve your English in your free time after school. Now your English teacher has asked you to write a report describing different ways to improve your English in your free time **and** saying which one you think is the best and why.

   Write your **report**.

5   Answer **one** of the following two questions based on **one** of the titles below.

   (a) *Phantom of the Opera* by Gaston Leroux
   You have been discussing the characters in *Phantom of the Opera* in your English class. Now your teacher has asked you to write this essay for homework:

   Who do you think is the most unhappy character in *Phantom of the Opera*? Write an essay giving your opinion.

   Write your **essay**.

   (b) *Great Expectations* by Charles Dickens
   This is part of a letter from your English penfriend, Kim:

   > *I thought the convict, Abel Magwitch, was a really bad man at the start of 'Great Expectations', but I changed my mind when I read the rest of the story. What did you think of him?*
   >
   > *Kim*

   Write your **letter**.

Test 3

PAPER 3   USE OF ENGLISH (45 minutes)

Part 1

For questions **1–12**, read the text below and decide which answer (**A, B, C** or **D**) best fits each gap. There is an example at the beginning (**0**).

Mark your answers **on the separate answer sheet**.

Example:

0   **A** suppose   **B** consider   **C** imagine   **D** think

0	A	B	C	D
			■	

A long snooze

Many people enjoy lying in bed in the morning, but can you **(0)** ..... having to spend 90 days in bed? Could you **(1)** ..... the boredom and the frustration of not being **(2)** ..... to get up? That was the **(3)** ..... that faced 14 volunteers when they **(4)** ..... on a bed-rest experiment being **(5)** ..... by the European Space Agency.

The study had a serious purpose: to **(6)** ..... the changes that take place in the human body during long-duration spaceflight. Lying in a horizontal position was the best way of simulating weightlessness. The aim was to discover what effect **(7)** ..... of weightlessness will have on the health of astronauts spending several months on the International Space Station.

The volunteers ate their meals, took showers and underwent medical tests without ever sitting up. That's even **(8)** ..... than it sounds, especially when you **(9)** ..... that no visitors were permitted. However, each volunteer did have a mobile phone, as well as **(10)** ..... to the latest films, computer games and music.

Surprisingly, everyone was in a good **(11)** ..... at the end of the 90 days. 'I would do it again,' said one of the volunteers. 'It was disorientating, but we knew we were **(12)** ..... to medical research and space exploration.'

Paper 3 Use of English

1	A	stand	B	maintain	C	hold	D	support
2	A	enabled	B	allowed	C	granted	D	approved
3	A	business	B	work	C	occupation	D	task
4	A	came by	B	started out	C	took off	D	set up
5	A	produced	B	carried	C	conducted	D	applied
6	A	investigate	B	search	C	inquire	D	question
7	A	times	B	periods	C	stages	D	terms
8	A	stronger	B	firmer	C	greater	D	tougher
9	A	reckon	B	realise	C	regard	D	remark
10	A	access	B	convenience	C	availability	D	freedom
11	A	attitude	B	spirit	C	feeling	D	mood
12	A	donating	B	participating	C	contributing	D	delivering

Part 2

For questions **13–24**, read the text below and think of the word which best fits each gap. Use only **one** word in each gap. There is an example at the beginning (**0**).

Write your answers **IN CAPITAL LETTERS on the separate answer sheet**.

Example: **0** B E E N

History from the sea

An ancient ship has (**0**) .... discovered beneath the waters of the Mediterranean. The ship, (**13**) .... sank off the coast of Tunisia more than 2,300 years ago, is already giving historians fresh insights (**14**) .... trade and diet in the ancient world.

The remains of the ship (**15**) .... found last August on the final day of an expedition undertaken (**16**) .... American scientist Robin Asquith. Three of his team, (**17**) .... were using a miniature submarine to explore the seabed, spotted rows of storage jars and some rotted wood. (**18**) .... of the jars was brought to the surface by a diver, and inside it the scientists found bones belonging to freshwater fish, and some olive stones.

After examining the contents and design of the jar and other evidence, Dr Asquith concluded that the ship (**19**) .... been following a trade route when (**20**) .... sank, probably in a storm. He intends to return to the site of the shipwreck, 32 km from the coast, (**21**) .... that he can conduct further investigations. He hopes to excavate making use (**22**) .... a new robot that uses sound to make a computer plan of the wreck, and in this way create (**23**) .... accurate picture of (**24**) .... the ship looked like.

Part 3

For questions **25–34**, read the text below. Use the word given in capitals at the end of some of the lines to form a word that fits in the gap **in the same line**. There is an example at the beginning (**0**).

Write your answers **IN CAPITAL LETTERS** on the separate answer sheet.

Example: | 0 | R | E | C | O | G | N | I | T | I | O | N | | | | |

Sport in society

The position of sport in today's society has changed out of all **(0)** .... **RECOGNISE**
People no longer seem to think of sport as 'just a game' – to be watched
or played for the sake of **(25)** .... Instead, it has become big business **ENJOY**
worldwide. It has become accepted practice for **(26)** .... companies **LEAD**
to provide sponsorship. TV companies pay large sums of money to
screen important matches or **(27)** .... The result has been huge **COMPETE**
(28) .... rewards for athletes, some of whom are now very **FINANCE**
(29) ...., particularly top footballers, golfers and tennis players. In addition, **WEALTH**
it is not **(30)** .... for some athletes to receive large fees on top of their **USUAL**
salary, for advertising products or making personal appearances.

A trend towards shorter working hours means that people **(31)** .... tend **GENERAL**
to have more free time, both to watch and to take part in sporting activity;
sport has become a **(32)** .... part of the recreation industry that we now **SIGNIFY**
rely on to fill our leisure hours. **(33)** .... sport is a vital part of that industry, **PROFESSION**
providing **(34)** .... for millions of ordinary people all over the world. **PLEASE**

Part 4

For questions **35–42**, complete the second sentence so that it has a similar meaning to the first sentence, using the word given. **Do not change the word given**. You must use between **two** and **five** words, including the word given. Here is an example (**0**).

Example:

0   A very friendly taxi driver drove us into town.

   DRIVEN

   We .... a very friendly taxi driver.

The gap can be filled by the words 'were driven into town by', so you write:

Example: | **0** | *WERE DRIVEN INTO TOWN BY* |

Write **only** the missing words **IN CAPITAL LETTERS** on the separate answer sheet.

---

35   The last time I saw Tom was the day he got married in 1995.

   WEDDING

   I haven't .... day in 1995.

36   Although the main actor performed well, the critics didn't like the play.

   GOOD

   In spite .... by the main actor, the critics didn't like the play.

37   My uncle lives quite near the sea.

   AWAY

   My uncle does .... from the sea.

38   Chess was more complicated than the children had expected.

   SUCH

   The children had not expected chess to .... complicated game.

39 John only lost his way because he'd forgotten his map.

LOST

If John hadn't forgotten his map, ... his way.

40 It was up to Melissa to decide where the family would go for their holiday.

TAKE

Melissa had .... about where the family would go for their holiday.

41 Everyone said it had been my fault that we lost the match.

BLAMED

Everyone .... fact that we lost the match.

42 Peter regretted selling his sports car so cheaply.

WISHED

Peter .... his sports car for more money.

Test 3

PAPER 4 LISTENING (approximately 40 minutes)

Part 1

You will hear people talking in eight different situations. For questions **1–8**, choose the best answer (**A**, **B** or **C**).

1   You hear a man talking about a teacher.
    What did the teacher encourage him to do?

    A to read more widely

    B to do some acting

    C to travel abroad

2   You overhear a woman talking on the phone about her computer.
    Why is she complaining?

    A The computer hasn't been repaired properly.

    B A promise hasn't been kept.

    C The computer hasn't been returned on time.

3   You hear two friends talking about a new sports centre.
    What is the man's opinion of it?

    A It offers value for money.

    B It is conveniently located.

    C It provides opportunities for socialising.

4   You overhear a woman and a man talking at a railway station.
    What does the woman want to do?

    A change her travel arrangements

    B find out appropriate information

    C complain about the trip

Paper 4 Listening

5   You hear part of a lecture on the radio.
    What is the lecturer doing?

    A supporting an existing theory

    B putting forward a theory of his own

    C arguing against other scientists' theories

6   You overhear a woman telling a friend about something she attended recently at her local college.
    What is she describing?

    A a concert

    B a lesson

    C a talk

7   You overhear a man and a woman who used to study at the same school talking together.
    In the man's opinion, what was the woman like at school?

    A forgetful

    B lazy

    C untidy

8   You hear a tennis player talking about how he hurt himself.
    What does he think caused his injury?

    A lifting something before a game

    B failing to prepare himself for a game

    C playing a difficult shot during a game

67

Test 3

Part 2

You will hear a man called Jeremy Baker talking about different ways of travelling in northern Finland. For questions **9–18**, complete the sentences.

Travelling in northern Finland

On his dog sled, the command Jeremy used most often with the dogs was [9]

Jeremy's dogs could understand commands in Finnish and [10], as well as English.

When travelling by sled, Jeremy tried to focus on the [11] of the lead dog.

The lead dog is always intelligent and generally [12]

Each dog can pull a weight of [13]

Jeremy had to avoid getting hit by [14] when riding among trees.

At lunchtime, Jeremy's job was to get [15] for cooking.

To Jeremy, travelling on a skidoo is like being on a [16]

Jeremy liked the skidoo except for the fact that it was [17]

The good thing about riding a skidoo is that your [18] don't get cold.

Part 3

You will hear five different people talking about shopping for clothes. For questions **19–23**, choose from the list (**A–F**) what each speaker says. Use the letters only once. There is one extra letter which you do not need to use.

A	I often buy clothes I don't need.		
		Speaker 1	19
B	I admit I spend too much on clothes.		
		Speaker 2	20
C	I plan in advance the clothes I need to buy.		
		Speaker 3	21
D	I tend to become bored with clothes I buy.		
		Speaker 4	22
E	I dislike wasting time on shopping.		
		Speaker 5	23
F	I am uncertain about what suits me.		

Part 4

You will hear part of an interview with the actor and film director Charles Martin. For questions **24–30**, choose the best answer (**A, B** or **C**).

24 How did Charles feel about acting in the TV series called *Cowboys*?

   A worried he would never play a different part

   B delighted to have secure work for some years

   C surprised that he was earning quite a low salary

25 What does Charles say about the first film he acted in?

   A The work was not as enjoyable as he had expected.

   B The part involved travelling to a number of different countries.

   C The role was quite similar to another he had played.

26 Why did Charles decide to play Miguel in a very simple way?

   A He felt he knew how the character would behave.

   B He was trying to copy the actors in old silent films.

   C He had no choice because there was not much dialogue.

27 When Charles played the detective in the film *The Good Cop*, he

   A made use of his real feelings in the role.

   B was unhappy about the way his part developed.

   C showed that he could represent strong emotion in his acting.

28 In the first film he directed, Charles offered a part to John Dawson because he

   A hoped to get advice on how to direct it.

   B thought this would help his friend's career.

   C knew John had experience in comedy films.

Paper 4 Listening

29 For Charles, working with actors is like conducting an orchestra because

    A there needs to be a lot of time for actors to practise their parts.

    B it is not easy to get a group of actors to work together well.

    C good actors may interpret their parts in unexpected ways.

30 Why does Charles like to film just one or two versions of each scene?

    A It leads to a reduction in the overall costs.

    B It makes the team more confident and efficient.

    C It helps the actors to remember their lines better.

Test 3

Paper 5 SPEAKING (14 minutes)

You take the Speaking test with another candidate (possibly two candidates), referred to here as your partner. There are two examiners. One will speak to you and your partner and the other will be listening. Both examiners will award marks.

Part 1 (3 minutes)

The examiner asks you and your partner questions about yourselves. You may be asked about things like 'your home town', 'your interests', 'your career plans', etc.

Part 2 (a one-minute 'long turn' for each candidate, plus 20-second response from the second candidate)

The examiner gives you two photographs and asks you to talk about them for one minute. The examiner then asks your partner a question about your photographs and your partner responds briefly.

Then the examiner gives your partner two different photographs. Your partner talks about these photographs for one minute. This time the examiner asks you a question about your partner's photographs and you respond briefly.

Part 3 (approximately 3 minutes)

The examiner asks you and your partner to talk together. You may be asked to solve a problem or try to come to a decision about something. For example, you might be asked to decide the best way to use some rooms in a language school. The examiner gives you a picture to help you but does not join in the conversation.

Part 4 (approximately 4 minutes)

The examiner asks some further questions, which leads to a more general discussion of what you have talked about in Part 3. You may comment on your partner's answers if you wish.

Test 4

Test 4

PAPER 1   READING (1 hour)

Part 1

You are going to read a magazine article about a woman called Clare Hall who used to train racehorses in Britain. For questions **1–8**, choose the answer (**A**, **B**, **C** or **D**) which you think fits best according to the text.

Mark your answers **on the separate answer sheet**.

A change of lifestyle

An allergy made Clare Hall give up her job training racehorses, but she has now created a new career for herself as a best-selling author. Jane Henman interviews her.

In the large field which would normally contain horses, there are three big dogs running wildly around. As I talk to Clare Hall and her husband, Daniel, he says, 'I'm not allowing Clare to have anything larger than those dogs.' It's said with a smile, but persuading one of Britain's most successful racehorse trainers to give up her work can't have been easy. Clare explains her situation: 'I'd been ill for some time, and then I discovered that I had actually developed an allergy to horses. Giving up training horses after so long was a horrible decision to take. But it wasn't as if I needed the money any more. And at least it allowed me to try writing on a full-time basis – I'd been scribbling away in my free time for years!'

Clare was brought up on a small farm. Her father couldn't afford to hire any farm workers so Clare was expected to take her share of the workload. 'One of my earliest jobs was to carry the lamp for my father when he went to feed the pigs at night. I remember feeling really grown up the day I was allowed to feed them on my own.' Sometimes Clare accompanied her father to the fields on her pony: 'I was little then and not confident on a horse. My father used to run alongside shouting, "Up, down, up, down."' As soon as she could, Clare got a weekend job at the local racing stables to be with the horses. Then, after leaving school, she worked at the stables full-time. Her parents were always supportive: 'They were there if I needed them, *line 29* but thankfully they took a back seat,' she says.

Clare's career as a trainer is legendary. She was not afraid of upsetting people and had a reputation for being outspoken. 'I have endless patience with horses – they respond to kindness and are prepared to work just as hard as you are – but I've no time for people who are in horse-racing purely for financial gain. The old, established trainers were helpful, but some of the rich newcomers were really spiteful and resented my success. I had my battles. But when everyone knew I was leaving, I was quite taken aback by the number of people who said, "Clare – you can't go!"'

Since giving up racehorse training, Clare has made a new career as a novelist. She writes laboriously in longhand at the dining-room table. 'Writing is a challenge but also very isolating,' Clare says. 'When I started, I had all the feelings I used to get before an important race – fear, apprehension, but that all disappears when you win or you're published!'

Clare's son Tim has now taken over her training business, keeping eighty of her horses. Despite the fact that Tim's only been doing this for two years, Clare announces proudly that he's already had several winners. 'But racehorse owners have high expectations. Keeping them happy is not an easy task,' she says. 'It is something you really have to work at *line 54* and I just hope he can cope.' She sometimes visits Tim's stables – not just to see the horses, but to see her granddaughter, who is also crazy about horses. 'Tim and his family come over here every Sunday and we talk about everything except horses, as I feel he needs a break from that,' she says.

Clare says she is trying to put her life in horse-racing behind her, but in the next breath, she's talking about a young horse at Tim's stables. There are compensations in her new lifestyle, however, such as more time to relax. 'My books are selling and I'm having golf lessons three times a week,' she says, smiling. 'We do need to sort things out better, though, so we have time to take holidays, and enjoy our hard-earned money!' However, as hard as she tries, there is obviously a huge gap in Clare's life that has yet to be filled.

Paper 1 Reading

1   What do we learn about Clare in the first paragraph?
    A   She is still worried about her financial security.
    B   She likes to follow her husband's advice.
    C   She was relieved to begin a less stressful job.
    D   She accepted that a change of career would be beneficial.

2   When Clare was a child, she
    A   was annoyed by her father's advice.
    B   was keen to earn money.
    C   enjoyed taking on responsibility.
    D   wanted to be more independent.

3   What does Clare mean by 'they took a back seat' in line 29?
    A   They gave her confidence.
    B   They had high expectations of her.
    C   They did not try to influence her.
    D   They did not ask her for help.

4   How did Clare feel at the end of her career as a trainer?
    A   upset by some people's personal criticism
    B   surprised at her colleagues' reactions
    C   relieved that the hard work was over
    D   proud of her contribution to horse-racing

5   According to Clare, horse training resembles writing in terms of
    A   the amount of effort required.
    B   the experience needed to succeed.
    C   the loneliness of the activity.
    D   the extremes of emotion involved.

6   What is Clare's attitude to her son?
    A   She considers that he is too competitive.
    B   She worries that he is under too much pressure.
    C   She believes that she should have more contact with him.
    D   She thinks he should spend more time with his daughter.

7   What does 'It' in line 54 refer to?
    A   dealing with the owners
    B   running a racing stable
    C   being successful in races
    D   earning money in horse-racing

8   In the final paragraph, the writer suggests that Clare
    A   plans to return to the horse-racing business.
    B   is exaggerating the size of her income.
    C   misses her involvement with horses.
    D   is concentrating too much on her hobbies.

75

Part 2

You are going to read a magazine article about a cruise ship. Seven sentences have been removed from the article. Choose from the sentences **A–H** the one which fits each gap (**9–15**). There is one extra sentence which you do not need to use.

Mark your answers **on the separate answer sheet**.

The *Oriana* turnaround

When the cruise ship *Oriana* comes into port, it has just 12 hours to get everything ready for the 1,800 passengers on its next cruise.
Chris Mersea joined the team for the day.

It's 6.00 a.m., still dark, and above the rooftops of the port city of Southampton a large orange funnel suddenly appears. It's attached to the 69,000-tonne cruise ship *Oriana*, the pride of P&O Cruise Lines. *Oriana* has been home, for the past eleven days, to some 1,800 passengers. It will soon be home to 1,800 different passengers yet to arrive in Southampton, but who in twelve hours' time will be setting sail for the Atlantic islands of Madeira and Tenerife.

In most small hotels the staff complain if they have to change more than ten bedrooms in one day. On *Oriana*, there are 900 cabins to be cleaned in just a few hours. **9**

On board *Oriana*, however, working practices are shaped not by the attitude of individual members of the staff, but by time, tide and a rigid cruise schedule. **10**

The first aim of the day is to have the last passengers off the ship and away by 10.30 a.m. **11** Even so, passengers manage to drive off home having forgotten sunglasses, souvenirs and even pearl earrings. The staff often find jewellery that has fallen down the backs of beds and chairs, and at least one passenger always manages to arrive home without his house keys – by which time the ship could already be halfway back across the Atlantic.

While *Oriana*'s armies of cabin stewards are changing sheets and looking for lost property, an enormous amount of activity is also taking place elsewhere on the ship. **12** Everything from 10 tonnes of fish, to 108 new sun chairs, to a vanload of scenery for the ship's Rio Dance Spectacular has to be carefully checked in.

The biggest problems of the day are a set of waiters' uniforms that have disappeared and several thousand boiled sweets that don't seem to have turned up. **13**

While all this is going on, there is also a large number of people coming and going. Turnaround day, according to the captain, starts off with an end-of-term feeling because a lot of the crew are saying goodbye, but then others are arriving to take their places. **14** These include a replacement head waiter, a new swimming-pool attendant and a new piano act called the Bibby Sisters, who will contribute to the ship's entertainment programme during the cruise.

For the moment, though, the priority is to meet and greet the new passengers, who start coming on board as early as 1.30 p.m. **15** Five hours later, back on dry land, the band will be playing their own version of *Sailing*, as *Oriana* heads out towards the open sea. It's a thrilling moment for the 1,800 men, women and children on board, who can look forward to eleven days of fun and relaxation.

A It's a leisurely process – nobody is made to feel they have to rush their goodbyes or their packing.

B Lorries full of supplies for the ship's stores are waiting to be unloaded.

C Hopefully, they haven't been missed amongst the loads of cornflakes and crisps that keep on coming, steered through the narrow corridors by dock workers in orange overalls.

D As for having to stock up on food for a fortnight ahead, no hotel chef would hear of it.

E These are entertained in the Tiffany Lounge area by a small group of musicians, playing pieces vaguely connected with the sea.

F Every so often, however, a loud crash announces the departure of another empty metal container.

G And today is no exception – in all, some 91 people are taking up or leaving their posts.

H It would take really extreme weather conditions to stop the ship departing and returning at the stated times, wherever it's sailing.

Test 4

Part 3

You are going to read an article in which four young people are talking about sport. For questions **16–30**, choose from the people (**A–D**). The people may be chosen more than once.

Mark your answers **on the separate answer sheet**.

Which person

thinks winning is the most important thing?	16
was inspired by seeing others take part in the sport?	17
feels their sport has both a positive and negative impact on their social life?	18
thinks that their sport may be inappropriate for a particular group of people?	19
was nearly refused a place on a team?	20
has changed their mind about participating in competitive sport?	21
has long-term plans which include continued involvement in their sport?	22
is realistic about their chances of being very successful?	23
feels that there is too much emphasis on analysing performance?	24
has learnt to be more sympathetic to less successful competitors?	25
thinks playing their sport changes their character?	26
uses a second sport to improve performance in their main sport?	27
is looking forward to a new challenge?	28
has friends locally who share their passion for sport?	29
thinks it is easier to perform well in their sport when they are calm?	30

Young people and sport

A Luke Hazleton

My mum is the team manager for the Olympic diving team and when I was a baby I used to go with her to the pool and jump in and out – now I practise diving every day after school and on Saturdays. I'm really too tall to be a great diver and my long legs make it difficult to do somersaults, so I don't think I'll ever make it to the top. But nevertheless, I find it exhilarating when I'm diving well. If it's a complicated dive, I have to concentrate very hard, which is difficult if I feel nervous. My dad's support is very motivating for me. I take part in about ten competitions a year, both national and international. The best thing about it is that you make new friends from different countries. I do trampolining for the regional team, which prepares me for diving – the moves are similar but you don't land in water! The one thing I don't like about it is that doing my homework takes up my spare time and I don't have much time to go out with my friends from school.

B Natalie Harris

Last year our netball team was promoted to the top league and so the coach became very strict. At that level, every move is scrutinised and discussed, which makes everyone feel very pressurised. There's a lot of competition to get chosen for the team and sometimes I got substituted. When I played last year, I would look at the subs sitting on the sidelines and not really care, but when I started to become one myself I had a whole new perspective on the game. Now I realise that when you're not the best at a sport it doesn't seem as much fun as when you're a top player. I left the team earlier this year, as the pressure of playing in matches was too much; it was becoming a frustration instead of a recreation. I still enjoy playing netball with my friends in gym classes, when I can relax without worrying about impressing my coach all the time.

C Joanne Whittaker

I was good at football and I really enjoyed playing left back in the school team. Then one Saturday when I was 14, I went to watch the local ice hockey team play. It was so exciting and became a real turning point in my life. School football seemed so dull in comparison. I discovered that there was a local women's ice hockey team just being set up. At first, the coach thought I was too young and too inexperienced as I'd only done occasional fun skating on Saturday afternoons. But she agreed to give me a trial and I have been playing for three years now. I'll really find out what I can do in June when we go to take part in a women's international ice hockey competition in Prague.

D James Spiers

I knew I was serious about rugby when I scored a try in my first game. I was named 'player of the year' at my club last year and I'm also captain of my school team. My uncle often comes to watch me play. He's very competitive so that is probably why I am too. Losing makes me feel that I've done something wrong. It doesn't happen very often, though. I'm not normally an aggressive person but, on the rugby pitch, I am. I don't think girls should play rugby as it's so aggressive and they could easily get injured. Most of my schoolmates play rugby and all of them are sporty. I can't really imagine my life without rugby! I'm going to agricultural college when I leave school and eventually will take over my uncle's farm, but I hope there'll still be time for lots of rugby. If I have a son, I'll want to help coach his team and I'd be disappointed if he wasn't interested in sports. I'll definitely be a competitive dad!

PAPER 2　WRITING (1 hour 20 minutes)

Part 1

You **must** answer this question. Write your answer in **120–150** words in an appropriate style.

1. You are helping your friend Anna arrange an end-of-year party at the international college where you study. Read Anna's email and the notes you have made. Then write an email to Anna using **all** your notes.

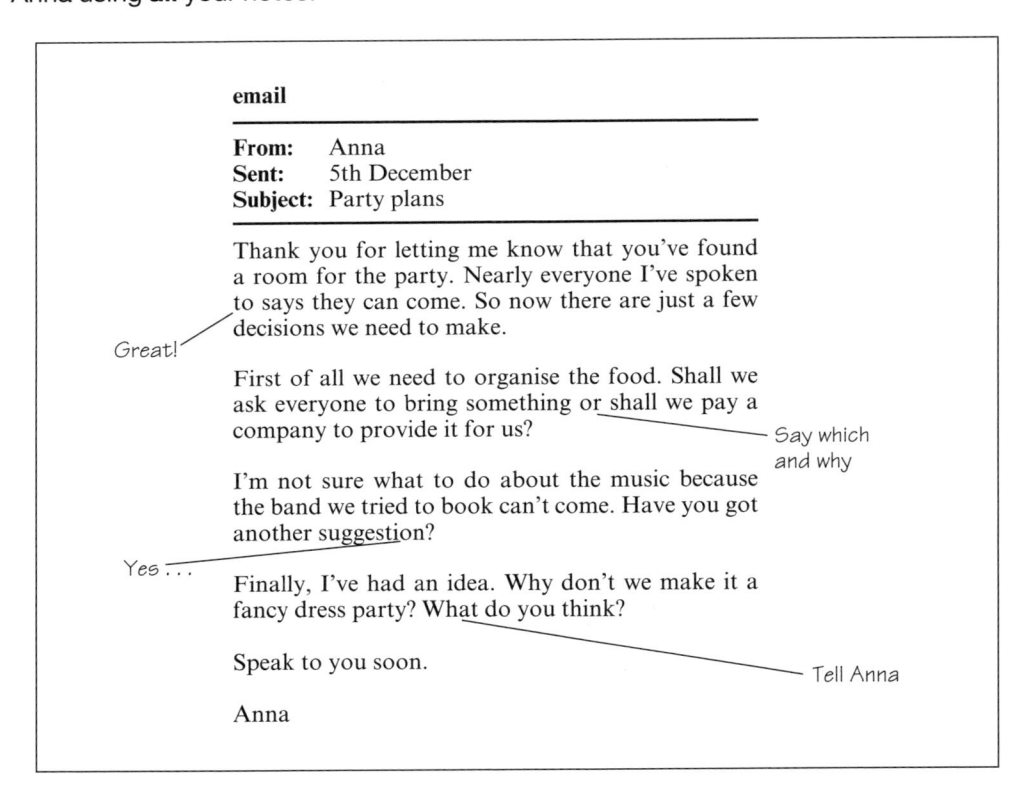

---

email

From: Anna
Sent: 5th December
Subject: Party plans

Thank you for letting me know that you've found a room for the party. Nearly everyone I've spoken to says they can come. So now there are just a few decisions we need to make. — *Great!*

First of all we need to organise the food. Shall we ask everyone to bring something or shall we pay a company to provide it for us? — *Say which and why*

I'm not sure what to do about the music because the band we tried to book can't come. Have you got another suggestion? — *Yes ...*

Finally, I've had an idea. Why don't we make it a fancy dress party? What do you think? — *Tell Anna*

Speak to you soon.

Anna

Write your **email**. You must use grammatically correct sentences with accurate spelling and punctuation in a style appropriate for the situation.

Visual materials for the Speaking test

- Why do people go to places like these for a day out?

1A

1B

C1

Visual materials for the Speaking test

- Why would people keep these photographs?
- Which photograph is the most special?

1E

Visual materials for the Speaking test

C3

Visual materials for the Speaking test

- What are the people enjoying about spending time in these different streets?

1C

1D

C4

Visual materials for the Speaking test

- Why are the people playing music in these places?

2A

2B

C5

Visual materials for the Speaking test

- What would people find easy or difficult about these activities?
- Which two activities would be most popular with people who don't usually do much exercise?

2E

Visual materials for the Speaking test

C7

Visual materials for the Speaking test

- Why is water important to these different people?

2C

2D

Visual materials for the Speaking test

- How useful is it for children to learn these things?

3A

3B

Visual materials for the Speaking test

- How suitable would the different activities be for people of different ages?
- Which two activities would be most popular with people of all ages?

3E

CAMPING

C10

Visual materials for the Speaking test

Visual materials for the Speaking test

- Why are the people taking a break in these places?

3C

3D

Visual materials for the Speaking test

- Why are the people travelling in these different ways?

4A

4B

Visual materials for the Speaking test

- Why is it good for people to have friends in these situations?
- In which situation is it most important to have friends?

4E

Visual materials for the Speaking test

C15

Visual materials for the Speaking test

- What can be difficult about doing these things?

4C

4D

Paper 2 Writing

Part 2

Write an answer to **one** of the questions **2–5** in this part. Write your answer in **120–180** words in an appropriate style.

2   Your English class has been discussing how useful different subjects studied at school are. Now your teacher has asked you to write an essay answering this question:

Which **two** subjects studied at school are most useful for our future lives?

Write your **essay**.

3   You see this advertisement in an international student magazine:

> **Holiday hire shop on the beach**
> We provide equipment for tourists to hire – bicycles, swimming and sports equipment.
> We need an English-speaking person to help in the shop who:
>
> - likes meeting people
> - is interested in sport
> - can advise on the equipment.
>
> Write and tell us why you are suitable for the job. Contact Mr James Carlton, Manager.

Write your **letter of application**.

4   Your teacher has asked you to write a story for the college English language magazine. The story must **begin** with the following words:

It all began when I found an old key at the back of the kitchen cupboard.

Write your **story**.

5   Answer **one** of the following two questions based on **one** of the titles below.

(a) *Great Expectations* by Charles Dickens
Your English teacher has given you this essay for homework:

Pip's life suddenly changes when he becomes rich. Does this money make him happy?

Write your **essay**.

(b) *Phantom of the Opera* by Gaston Leroux
This is part of a letter you have received from your English-speaking penfriend, Robin:

> *I really enjoyed 'Phantom of the Opera', but can you explain why Erik allowed Christine to leave and marry Raoul? I thought Erik wanted to keep her for himself . . .*
>
> *Write soon.*
>
> *Robin*

Write your **letter**.

Test 4

PAPER 3   USE OF ENGLISH (45 minutes)

Part 1

For questions **1–12**, read the text below and decide which answer (**A, B, C** or **D**) best fits each gap. There is an example at the beginning (**0**).

Mark your answers **on the separate answer sheet**.

Example:

0   **A** follow   **B** belong   **C** own   **D** hold

0	A	B	C	D
		■		

Dogs

Dogs were one of the first animals to be domesticated. Although they all **(0)** ..... to the same species, they **(1)** ..... more in size and appearance than any other animal, and are now **(2)** ..... wherever there are human beings. They all have good hearing and an excellent sense of smell. **(3)** ..... the differences between breeds, all dogs are **(4)** ..... from the same ancestor, the grey wolf. Wolves enjoy hunting and are ready to run **(5)** ..... prey, which is why dogs today like energetic games and plenty of exercise. Pet dogs that are not **(6)** ..... enough to do can become bored and **(7)** ..... . Like wolves, dogs lived in groups called packs. They **(8)** ..... well to domestication as they came to **(9)** ..... their human owners as pack leaders.

The domestication of dogs began many thousands of years ago when grey wolves, in search of food, were **(10)** ..... to human settlements. The wolves must gradually have become used to people, who would soon have discovered that they were quite useful animals, for wolves ran faster than people and could **(11)** ..... them hunt other animals. People **(12)** ..... for the wild wolves and so the wolves became domesticated.

82

1	A	transform	B	alter	C	change	D	vary
2	A	general	B	average	C	common	D	ordinary
3	A	Despite	B	Although	C	However	D	While
4	A	emerged	B	linked	C	descended	D	related
5	A	away	B	after	C	into	D	over
6	A	given	B	provided	C	handed	D	presented
7	A	destructive	B	harmful	C	damaging	D	injuring
8	A	suited	B	grew	C	responded	D	matched
9	A	think	B	see	C	agree	D	believe
10	A	interested	B	attracted	C	appealed	D	tempted
11	A	assist	B	help	C	support	D	allow
12	A	guarded	B	protected	C	attended	D	cared

Part 2

For questions **13–24**, read the text below and think of the word which best fits each gap. Use only **one** word in each gap. There is an example at the beginning (**0**).

Write your answers **IN CAPITAL LETTERS on the separate answer sheet**.

Example: | 0 | H | A | S |

A hotel famous for its food

The Riverside Hotel **(0)** .... had a reputation for excellent food ever **(13)** .... the day it opened in 1949. In the previous year, a businessman called Henry Davies was reading a newspaper when he suddenly **(14)** .... across an advertisement showing a house **(15)** .... sale overlooking a river. The advertisement interested him because for several years he had been thinking **(16)** .... converting a family home **(17)** .... a hotel. The house seemed to be exactly **(18)** .... he was looking for.

Davies **(19)** .... soon running the hotel himself, but hired a top chef, Geoffrey Dawson, to be in charge of the cooking. Within six months, the restaurant was **(20)** .... heavily booked that Davies had to take on new kitchen staff. The partnership lasted for almost 50 years. During **(21)** .... time, the hotel won several awards for the quality of its food.

Today, in the hotel business, the names Davies and Dawson are still held in considerable respect. Indeed, **(22)** .... the years, the Riverside Hotel has inspired many other hotel owners **(23)** .... create similar hotels. Under the present owner, Sally Rutland, the excellence of the food remains unchanged, and Sally has personally trained **(24)** .... number of chefs who have gone on to become famous in their field.

Part 3

For questions **25–34**, read the text below. Use the word given in capitals at the end of some of the lines to form a word that fits in the gap **in the same line**. There is an example at the beginning (**0**).

Write your answers **IN CAPITAL LETTERS** on the separate answer sheet.

Example: | 0 | F | I | T | N | E | S | S | | | | | | | |

Running for health

If you want to improve your overall level of (0) .... , running is one of the **FIT**
best sports to choose. It can increase the (25) .... of your bones, it is good **STRONG**
for your heart, and it can help with weight (26) .... You will soon begin **LOSE**
to see a (27) .... improvement in your general health and if you are the **SIGNIFY**
sort of person who enjoys a challenge, then you could consider making the
(28) .... to run a marathon – a race of approximately 42 kilometres. **DECIDE**

Experienced runners and sports (29) .... say you should make a point **INSTRUCT**
of having a physical check-up with your doctor before you start training.
Another (30) .... is that anyone who has an old back, knee or ankle **RECOMMEND**
(31) .... should take extra care. You should never use running shoes **INJURE**
which hurt your feet or which feel (32) .... after a long run. It is a good **COMFORT**
idea to start by running slowly for about twenty minutes three times a week
and (33) .... increase the number of kilometres you run. You should find **GRADUAL**
running long (34) .... gets progressively easier, and after a time, you may **DISTANT**
feel that even a marathon will be possible!

Part 4

For questions **35–42**, complete the second sentence so that it has a similar meaning to the first sentence, using the word given. **Do not change the word given**. You must use between **two** and **five** words, including the word given. Here is an example (**0**).

Example:

0   A very friendly taxi driver drove us into town.

   DRIVEN

   We .... a very friendly taxi driver.

The gap can be filled by the words 'were driven into town by', so you write:

Example: | **0** | WERE DRIVEN INTO TOWN BY |

Write **only** the missing words **IN CAPITAL LETTERS on the separate answer sheet**.

---

35   You shouldn't take any notice of his advice.

   LISTEN

   If I were you, ... his advice.

36   Naomi is the only person who wants to go to the cinema tonight.

   NOBODY

   Apart .... interested in going to the cinema tonight.

37   'What is the depth of the pool?' the woman asked.

   HOW

   The woman asked .... was.

38   They are demolishing the old town hall on Friday.

   PULLED

   The old town hall is to .... on Friday.

39 I am absolutely sure we will win the match tomorrow.

DOUBT

There's absolutely .... mind that we will win the match tomorrow.

40 'Would it be possible to see a copy of the latest bus timetable, please?' said Joan.

COULD

Joan asked .... at a copy of the latest bus timetable.

41 Leah suggested that I arrive on time for the presentation.

LATE

Leah advised .... for the presentation.

42 I was angry when Sandra was rude to me this morning.

MADE

Sandra's rudeness .... my temper this morning.

Test 4

PAPER 4 LISTENING (approximately 40 minutes)

Part 1

You will hear people talking in eight different situations. For questions **1–8**, choose the best answer (**A**, **B** or **C**).

1   You hear a young fashion model talking about the first magazine feature she appeared in.
    Why were she and her sister chosen for the feature?

    A   They were willing to change their hair colour.

    B   They looked very similar to each other.

    C   They looked good in the designer clothes.

2   You hear a woman on the radio talking about her experiences at ballet school.
    How did she feel when she left the school?

    A   relieved

    B   embarrassed

    C   depressed

3   You hear a student talking about a part-time job he does.
    What attracted him to this particular job?

    A   the opportunities for promotion

    B   the chance to use skills he already had

    C   the amount of money he is able to earn

4   You overhear a man and a woman talking about a ride at a theme park.
    What does the man say about the ride?

    A   It was too short.

    B   It was too expensive.

    C   It was too frightening.

Paper 4 Listening

5 You hear an announcement at the train station.
   Who would find this announcement relevant?

   A passengers waiting for the train from Wellington

   B passengers waiting to board the Hamilton train

   C passengers waiting on platform 4

6 You overhear two people in a clothes shop talking about some trousers.
   What do they both like?

   A the style

   B the colour

   C the material

7 You overhear a teacher talking to her students.
   What is she doing?

   A advising them of room changes

   B informing them about additional classes

   C explaining about new tutor group meeting times

8 You hear part of a radio interview with a rock musician who is performing in his home town.
   What do the two speakers agree about?

   A Tickets for rock concerts in the town are expensive.

   B There is a lack of suitable venues in the town.

   C The music scene in the town is very lively.

Part 2

You will hear an interview with a man called Lucas Doran, who is talking about his job as a zookeeper. For questions **9–18**, complete the sentences.

Zookeeper

Lucas used to enjoy looking after the [__9__] when he first worked at the zoo.

Every morning, Lucas checks to see if any monkeys are [__10__] or if any babies have been born.

Every morning, Lucas also cleans the monkeys' cages and replaces the [__11__].

The monkeys eat many different things, but are especially fond of [__12__].

Lucas once injured his [__13__] when a gorilla escaped from its cage.

Lucas particularly likes talking to the [__14__] who come to the zoo.

Lucas says that giving the monkeys food such as [__15__] is unsuitable.

Lucas once took a box of baby monkeys home by [__16__].

Lucas is now taking a course in [__17__] so that he can further his career.

Lucas's ambition is to visit a [__18__] for wild animals in Africa to see the work done there.

Part 3

You will hear five different people talking about taking photographs. For questions **19–23**, choose from the list (**A–F**) the subject that each person is most interested in photographing. Use the letters only once. There is one extra letter which you do not need to use.

A	news stories		
		Speaker 1	19
B	celebrities		
		Speaker 2	20
C	sports events		
		Speaker 3	21
D	holidays		
		Speaker 4	22
E	nature		
		Speaker 5	23
F	family scenes		

Test 4

Part 4

You will hear a radio interview with two students, Annabelle Lester and Roberto Marini, who are both studying at the same art school. For questions **24–30**, choose the best answer (**A, B** or **C**).

24 Annabelle enjoys studying at Capital Art School because

   A she has plenty of time to practise different skills.

   B she is learning how to create a range of different things.

   C she is able to do a full-time course in sculpture and painting.

25 What does Roberto say about the lectures on his course?

   A Some are given by business people.

   B Some of the best ones are about art history.

   C Some are held in the studios of professional artists.

26 Annabelle says she chose to study at Capital Art School because

   A the students do not have to pay fees for the course.

   B the college provides all the materials that are needed.

   C the students are encouraged to try out new ideas.

27 Roberto says that his course includes learning how to

   A compare everyday objects and works of art.

   B produce magazine illustrations and advertisements.

   C improve the design of domestic equipment.

28 Roberto uses a computer to

   A complete a piece of artwork.

   B put together some initial ideas.

   C write up his project.

29 Annabelle says that some of the school's technical equipment

    A was lent by a local business.

    B is too complicated for students to operate.

    C is supplied by a company that likes students to test it.

30 What does Annabelle say about her future?

    A She looks forward to teaching art.

    B She would be willing to work in industry.

    C She is not keen to get a job in an art gallery.

Test 4

Paper 5 SPEAKING (14 minutes)

You take the Speaking test with another candidate (possibly two candidates), referred to here as your partner. There are two examiners. One will speak to you and your partner and the other will be listening. Both examiners will award marks.

Part 1 (3 minutes)

The examiner asks you and your partner questions about yourselves. You may be asked about things like 'your home town', 'your interests', 'your career plans', etc.

Part 2 (a one-minute 'long turn' for each candidate, plus 20-second response from the second candidate)

The examiner gives you two photographs and asks you to talk about them for one minute. The examiner then asks your partner a question about your photographs and your partner responds briefly.

Then the examiner gives your partner two different photographs. Your partner talks about these photographs for one minute. This time the examiner asks you a question about your partner's photographs and you respond briefly.

Part 3 (approximately 3 minutes)

The examiner asks you and your partner to talk together. You may be asked to solve a problem or try to come to a decision about something. For example, you might be asked to decide the best way to use some rooms in a language school. The examiner gives you a picture to help you but does not join in the conversation.

Part 4 (approximately 4 minutes)

The examiner asks some further questions, which leads to a more general discussion of what you have talked about in Part 3. You may comment on your partner's answers if you wish.

Paper 5 frames

Test 1

Note: In the examination, there will be both an assessor and an interlocutor in the room.
The visual material for **Test 1** appears on pages C1 and C4 (Part 2), and C2–C3 (Part 3).

Part 1   3 minutes (5 minutes for groups of three)

Interlocutor: Good morning/afternoon/evening. My name is .... and this is my colleague ....
And your names are?
Can I have your mark sheets, please?
Thank you.
First of all, we'd like to know something about you.

- Where are you from, *(Candidate A)*?
- And you, *(Candidate B)*?
- What do you like about living *(here / name of candidate's home town)*?
- And what about you, *(Candidate A/B)*?

Select one or more questions from any of the following categories, as appropriate.

Leisure and entertainment
- What sort of films do you prefer to watch? ...... (Why?)
- Tell us about the last time you went shopping.

Media
- Do you like any magazines? ...... (Which ones?)
- Do you use the internet to find out about the news? ...... (Why? / Why not?)

Future life
- Do you think your life will change much in the future? ...... (Why? / Why not?)
- Do you plan to use your English in the future? ...... (How?)

Paper 5 frames

Part 2 4 minutes (6 minutes for groups of three)

A day out
City streets

Interlocutor:	In this part of the test, I'm going to give each of you two photographs. I'd like you to talk about your photographs on your own for about a minute, and also to answer a short question about your partner's photographs.
	(Candidate A), it's your turn first. Here are your photographs. They show places where people go for a day out.
	Indicate pictures 1A and 1B on page C1 to Candidate A.
	I'd like you to compare the photographs, and say why you think people go to places like these for a day out. All right?
Candidate A:	[*1 minute.*]
Interlocutor:	Thank you.
	(Candidate B), which place would you prefer to visit?
Candidate B:	[*Approximately 20 seconds.*]
Interlocutor:	Thank you.
	Now, *(Candidate B)*, here are your photographs. They show streets in different cities.
	Indicate pictures 1C and 1D on page C4 to Candidate B.
	I'd like you to compare the photographs, and say what the people are enjoying about spending time in these different streets. All right?
Candidate B:	[*1 minute.*]
Interlocutor:	Thank you.
	(Candidate A), do you enjoy being in a city?
Candidate A:	[*Approximately 20 seconds.*]
Interlocutor:	Thank you.

Paper 5 frames

Parts 3 and 4 7 minutes (9 minutes for groups of three)

Part 3

Special photographs

Interlocutor:	Now, I'd like you to talk about something together for about three minutes. *(4 minutes for groups of three.)*
	People often keep photographs to remind themselves of special times in their lives. Here are some pictures that people have decided to keep.
	Indicate the set of pictures 1E on pages C2–C3 to the candidates.
	First, talk to each other about why you think people would keep these photographs. Then decide which photograph you think is the most special. All right?
Candidates:	[*3 minutes.*]
Interlocutor:	Thank you.

Part 4

Interlocutor: *Select any of the following questions, as appropriate:*

- What sort of photographs do you like to keep?
- Do you like it when people take photographs of you? ...... (Why? / Why not?)
- Why do you think some people are so interested in looking at photographs of famous people?
- What is the best way to remember places you've visited, taking photographs or buying souvenirs? ...... (Why?)
- Do you think it's a good idea to always take a camera with you on holiday? ...... (Why? / Why not?)
- Is it a good idea to keep a diary to help you remember special times? ...... (Why?)

Select any of the following prompts, as appropriate:

- What do you think?
- Do you agree?
- And you?

Thank you. That is the end of the test.

Paper 5 frames

Test 2

Note: In the examination, there will be both an assessor and an interlocutor in the room.
The visual material for **Test 2** appears on pages C5 and C8 (Part 2), and C6–C7 (Part 3).

Part 1   3 minutes (5 minutes for groups of three)

Interlocutor: Good morning/afternoon/evening. My name is .... and this is my colleague ....
And your names are?
Can I have your mark sheets, please?
Thank you.
First of all, we'd like to know something about you.

- Where are you from, *(Candidate A)*?
- And you, *(Candidate B)*?
- What do you like about living *(here / name of candidate's home town)*?
- And what about you, *(Candidate A/B)*?

Select one or more questions from any of the following categories, as appropriate.

Personal experience
- Tell us about the last meal you really enjoyed.
- What do you like most about your family? ...... (Why?)

Travel
- How do you prefer to travel? ...... (Why?)
- Do you have any travel plans for the future? ...... (Where are you going?)

Free time activity
- What's the most interesting thing you do in your free time? ...... (Why?)
- Do you spend a lot of time using a computer? ...... (Why? / Why not?)

Part 2 4 minutes (6 minutes for groups of three)
Music
Water

Interlocutor:	In this part of the test, I'm going to give each of you two photographs. I'd like you to talk about your photographs on your own for about a minute, and also to answer a short question about your partner's photographs.
	(Candidate A), it's your turn first. Here are your photographs. They show people playing music in different places.
	Indicate pictures 2A and 2B on page C5 to Candidate A.
	I'd like you to compare the photographs, and say why you think the people are playing music in these places. All right?
Candidate A:	[*1 minute.*]
Interlocutor:	Thank you.
	(Candidate B), do you play a musical instrument?
Candidate B:	[*Approximately 20 seconds.*]
Interlocutor:	Thank you.
	Now, *(Candidate B)*, here are your photographs. They show people using water in different ways.
	Indicate pictures 2C and 2D on page C8 to Candidate B.
	I'd like you to compare the photographs, and say why you think water is important to these different people. All right?
Candidate B:	[*1 minute.*]
Interlocutor:	Thank you.
	(Candidate A), who do you think is enjoying their time more?
Candidate A:	[*Approximately 20 seconds.*]
Interlocutor:	Thank you.

Paper 5 frames

Parts 3 and 4   7 minutes (9 minutes for groups of three)

Part 3

Sports centre

Interlocutor:	Now, I'd like you to talk about something together for about three minutes. *(4 minutes for groups of three.)*
	I'd like you to imagine that a sports centre wants to attract people who don't usually do much exercise. Here are some activities they are thinking about.
	Indicate the set of pictures 2E on pages C6–C7 to the candidates.
	First, talk to each other about what people would find easy or difficult about these activities. Then decide which two activities would be most popular with people who don't usually do much exercise. All right?
Candidates:	*[3 minutes.]*
Interlocutor:	Thank you.

Part 4

Interlocutor: *Select any of the following questions, as appropriate:*

- Do you ever go to a sports centre? ...... (What do you do there?)
- More and more people are going to sports centres these days. Why do you think this is?
- What do you think people like about belonging to clubs?
- Do you think children should be taught to play sports at school? ...... (Why? / Why not?)
- Why do you think famous sportsmen and women are popular with young people?
- Is it a good thing for a country to hold big international sporting events like the Olympic Games? ...... (Why? / Why not?)

Select any of the following prompts, as appropriate:

- What do you think?
- Do you agree?
- And you?

Thank you. That is the end of the test.

Paper 5 frames

Test 3

Note: In the examination, there will be both an assessor and an interlocutor in the room.
The visual material for **Test 3** appears on pages C9 and C12 (Part 2), and C10–C11 (Part 3).

Part 1 3 minutes (5 minutes for groups of three)

Interlocutor: Good morning/afternoon/evening. My name is .... and this is my colleague ....
And your names are?
Can I have your mark sheets, please?
Thank you.
First of all, we'd like to know something about you.

- Where are you from, *(Candidate A)*?
- And you, *(Candidate B)*?
- What do you like about living *(here / name of candidate's home town)*?
- And what about you, *(Candidate A/B)*?

Select one or more questions from any of the following categories, as appropriate.

Holidays
- Do you usually take books with you to read on holiday? ...... (Why? / Why not?)
- Is there a place in the world you would really like to visit? ...... (Why? / Why not?)

Likes and dislikes
- Which is your favourite month of the year? ...... (Why?)
- Do you like to plan your holidays a long time in advance? ...... (Why? / Why not?)

Sport
- Do you prefer to exercise with other people or on your own? ...... (Why?)
- Are any of your friends very good at sports? ...... (Which ones?)

Paper 5 frames

Part 2 4 minutes (6 minutes for groups of three)

Children learning
Taking a break

Interlocutor:	In this part of the test, I'm going to give each of you two photographs. I'd like you to talk about your photographs on your own for about a minute, and also to answer a short question about your partner's photographs.
	(Candidate A), it's your turn first. Here are your photographs. They show children learning different things.
	Indicate pictures 3A and 3B on page C9 to Candidate A.
	I'd like you to compare the photographs, and say how useful it is for children to learn these things. All right?
Candidate A:	[*1 minute.*]
Interlocutor:	Thank you.
	(Candidate B), do you enjoy studying mathematics?
Candidate B:	[*Approximately 20 seconds.*]
Interlocutor:	Thank you.
	Now, *(Candidate B)*, here are your photographs. They show people taking a break in different places.
	Indicate pictures 3C and 3D on page C12 to Candidate B.
	I'd like you to compare the photographs, and say why you think the people are taking a break in these places. All right?
Candidate B:	[*1 minute.*]
Interlocutor:	Thank you.
	(Candidate A), do you enjoy relaxing in the fresh air?
Candidate A:	[*Approximately 20 seconds.*]
Interlocutor:	Thank you.

Paper 5 frames

Parts 3 and 4 7 minutes (9 minutes for groups of three)

Part 3

Campsite

Interlocutor:	Now, I'd like you to talk about something together for about three minutes. *(4 minutes for groups of three.)* I'd like you to imagine that the owners of a campsite want to introduce some new activities to attract more people of different ages. Here are some ideas they are thinking about. *Indicate the set of pictures 3E on pages C10–C11 to the candidates.* First, talk to each other about how suitable the different activities would be for people of different ages. Then decide which two activities would be most popular with people of all ages. All right?
Candidates:	[*3 minutes.*]
Interlocutor:	Thank you.

Part 4

Interlocutor:	*Select any of the following questions, as appropriate:* • Would you like to go on a camping holiday? …… (Why? / Why not?) • Why do you think some people prefer camping to staying in a hotel? • What do you think are the disadvantages of a camping holiday? • At what age do you think parents should allow their children to go away on holiday on their own? …… (Why?) • Would you like to work in the tourist industry? …… (Why? / Why not?) • Do you think tourism is always a good thing for a country? …… (Why? / Why not?) Thank you. That is the end of the test.

Select any of the following prompts, as appropriate:

• What do you think?
• Do you agree?
• And you?

Paper 5 frames

Test 4

Note: In the examination, there will be both an assessor and an interlocutor in the room.
The visual material for **Test 4** appears on pages C13 and C16 (Part 2) and C14–C15 (Part 3).

Part 1   3 minutes (*5 minutes for groups of three*)

Interlocutor: Good morning/afternoon/evening. My name is .... and this is my colleague ....
And your names are?
Can I have your mark sheets, please?
Thank you.
First of all, we'd like to know something about you.

- Where are you from, *(Candidate A)*?
- And you, *(Candidate B)*?
- What do you like about living *(here / name of candidate's home town)*?
- And what about you, *(Candidate A/B)*?

Select one or more questions from any of the following categories, as appropriate.

Daily routine
- Do you have enough free time? ...... (Why? / Why not?)
- Do you watch television every day? ...... (How much television do you watch?)

Work and education
- Is there anything you would really like to study in the future? ...... (What?)
- Would you prefer to work inside or outside? ...... (Why?)

Music
- Do you like listening to the same music as your parents? ...... (Why? / Why not?)
- Is there a musical instrument you would really like to play? ...... (Why? / Why not?)

Paper 5 frames

Part 2 4 minutes (6 minutes for groups of three)

Travelling
Adventure activities

Interlocutor:	In this part of the test, I'm going to give each of you two photographs. I'd like you to talk about your photographs on your own for about a minute, and also to answer a short question about your partner's photographs.
	(Candidate A), it's your turn first. Here are your photographs. They show people travelling in different ways.
	Indicate pictures 4A and 4B on page C13 to Candidate A.
	I'd like you to compare the photographs, and say why you think the people are travelling in these different ways. All right?
Candidate A:	[*1 minute.*]
Interlocutor:	Thank you.
	(Candidate B), do you enjoy travelling by train?
Candidate B:	[*Approximately 20 seconds.*]
Interlocutor:	Thank you.
	Now, *(Candidate B)*, here are your photographs. They show people doing adventurous things.
	Indicate pictures 4C and 4D on page C16 to Candidate B.
	I'd like you to compare the photographs, and say what you think can be difficult about doing these things. All right?
Candidate B:	[*1 minute.*]
Interlocutor:	Thank you.
	(Candidate A), would you like to do either of these things?
Candidate A:	[*Approximately 20 seconds.*]
Interlocutor:	Thank you.

Paper 5 frames

Parts 3 and 4 7 minutes (9 minutes for groups of three)

Part 3

Having friends

Interlocutor: Now, I'd like you to talk about something together for about three minutes.
(4 minutes for groups of three.)

Here are some situations in which it's good for people to have friends.

Indicate the set of pictures 4E on pages C14–C15 to the candidates.

First, talk to each other about why it's good for people to have friends in these situations. Then decide in which situation it's most important to have friends. All right?

Candidates: [*3 minutes.*]

Interlocutor: Thank you.

Part 4

Interlocutor: *Select any of the following questions, as appropriate:*

- How are your friends similar to you and how are they different?
- How important do you think it is to have a 'best friend'? ...... (Why?)
- Do you think it's good for friends to share everything with each other? ...... (Why? / Why not?)
- What can you do to stay friends with someone when you live a long way away from them?
- Apart from friends, who can people go to when they need advice? ...... (Why?)
- Are there times when it's better to be alone? ...... (When?) ...... (Why?)

Select any of the following prompts, as appropriate:

- What do you think?
- Do you agree?
- And you?

Thank you. That is the end of the test.

Marks and results

Paper 1 Reading

Candidates record their answers on a separate answer sheet. Two marks are given for each correct answer in **Parts 1** and **2** and one mark is given for each correct answer in **Part 3**. The total score is then weighted to 40 marks for the whole Reading paper.

Paper 2 Writing

General Impression Mark Scheme

A General Impression Mark Scheme is used in conjunction with a Task-specific Mark Scheme, which focuses on criteria specific to each particular task. The General Impression Mark Scheme summarises the content, organisation and cohesion, range of structures and vocabulary, register and format, and target reader indicated in each task.

A summary of the General Impression Mark Scheme is given below. Trained examiners, who are co-ordinated prior to each examination session, work with a more detailed version, which is subject to updating. The FCE General Impression Mark Scheme is interpreted at Council of Europe Common European Framework Level B2.

Band 5	For a **Band 5** to be awarded, the candidate's writing fully achieves the desired effect on the target reader. All the content points required in the task are included* and expanded on appropriately. Ideas are organised effectively, with the use of a variety of linking devices and a wide range of structures and vocabulary. The language is well developed, and any errors that do occur are minimal and perhaps due to ambitious attempts at more complex language. Register and format are consistently appropriate to the purpose of the task and the audience.
Band 4	For a **Band 4** to be awarded, the candidate's writing achieves the desired effect on the target reader. All the content points required in the task are included.* Ideas are clearly organised, with the use of suitable linking devices and a good range of structures and vocabulary. Generally, the language is accurate, and any errors that do occur are mainly due to attempts at more complex language. Register and format are, on the whole, appropriate to the purpose of the task and the audience.
Band 3	For a **Band 3** to be awarded, the candidate's writing, on the whole, achieves the desired effect on the target reader. All the content points required in the task are included.* Ideas are organised adequately, with the use of simple linking devices and an adequate range of structures and vocabulary. A number of errors may be present but they do not impede communication. A reasonable, if not always successful, attempt is made at register and format which are appropriate to the purpose of the task and the audience.
Band 2	For a **Band 2** to be awarded, the candidate's writing does not clearly communicate the message to the target reader. Some content points required in the task are inadequately covered or omitted, and/or there is some irrelevant material. Ideas are inadequately organised, linking devices are rarely used, and the range of structures and vocabulary is limited. Errors distract the reader and may obscure communication at times. Attempts at appropriate register and format are unsuccessful or inconsistent.

Marks and results

Band 1	For a **Band 1** to be awarded, the candidate's writing has a very negative effect on the target reader. There is notable omission of content points and/or considerable irrelevance, possibly due to misinterpretation of the task. There is a lack of organisation or linking devices, and there is little evidence of language control. The range of structures and vocabulary is narrow and frequent errors obscure communication. There is little or no awareness of appropriate register and format.
Band 0	For a **Band zero** to be awarded, either there is too little language for assessment or the candidate's writing is totally irrelevant or totally illegible.

* Candidates who do not address all the content points will be penalised for dealing inadequately with the requirements of the task.
  Candidates who fully satisfy the **Band 3** descriptor are likely to demonstrate an adequate performance in writing at FCE level.

Paper 2 sample answers and examiner's comments

The following pieces of writing have been selected from students' answers. The samples relate to tasks in Tests 1–4. Explanatory notes have been added to show how the bands have been arrived at. The comments should be read in conjunction with the Task-specific Mark Schemes included in the Keys.

Sample A (Test 1, Question 5b – Article)

> While I am reading a book, I can find each of character has their own individuality. Most of them are like our neighbours. But a few of them are unique or rather strange.
>
> Miss Havisham in 'Great Expectations' was the strangest character for me. After she was decieved by her fiancée, she didn't get over and just thought it over in tragic. So eventually she decided to revenge to all man in the world by bring up Estella as a 'heartbreaker'. But because of this, she ruined herself and Estella also became unhappy without any belief of love.
>
> At first I couldn't understand her. Because even though she could see her future more positively, she decided to stay in depression. However somehow I could understand her after I finished reading the book. It was because nobody had given her love, so she couldn't live differently.
>
> In conclusion, the author described various lifestyles. Sometimes there is strange character like 'Miss Havisham'. But because it was all based on our lives, I think they also can be understandable.

Comments

Content
Reasonable achievement of the task set.

Organisation and cohesion
Reasonable attempt at organisation.

Range
An adequate range of structure and vocabulary.

Accuracy
A number of errors, some of which distract.

Appropriacy of register and format
Appropriate to the task.

Target reader
Would be informed.

Band: 3

Marks and results

Sample B (Test 2, Question 1 – Email)

> I'm really happy for this trip too! I think we'll have a great time there together! The house seems very nice, and I really love that it's near the countryside. For me, it's better to go in the next week, because these days I have a lot of works to do...
>
> I think the bicycles are better because it's a very good excersise and mostly it's envirohmentaly friendly. Also in the way, we would see better the nature.
>
> The location is wonderfull! We can go some walks to the maintain, we can climb, but we will also have silence, so we can rela and read some books into the house. But if we want to have some fun at night, we can go to the centre, can't we?
>
> I would like to know if there is a fireplace in the house because I'm a bit of sick these days, and that would help me.
>
> I'm waiting for your answers,
>
> Love,

Comments

Content
All content points included.

Organisation and cohesion
Ideas clearly organised.

Range
Adequate range of structure and vocabulary.

Accuracy
A number of non-impeding errors.

Appropriacy of register and format
Appropriate for the task.

Target reader
Would be informed.

Band: 3

Sample C (Test 2, Question 3 – Story)

> Mark opened the envelope, read the letter and immediately started to pack his bag. He was so excited. We really hoped he would win the competition from the moment he read the magazine.
>
> That night was extremely long for Mark. He was so impatient that he couldn't sleep. He kept looking at the clock. He was going to meet her and he still couldn't believe it! In the morning he ate his breakfast and then he waited outside his house. According to the letter the limousine would arrive at 10:00 and so it happened.
>
> He had won the greatest prize ever. He would spend the weekend in the most luxurius hotel in New York and he would have a meal with Kelly Clarkson a famous singer and the girl of his dreams.
>
> On Saturday he had a bath on his luxurius bathroom and then he had a tour on the city.
>
> It was Sunday afternoon. He was standing outside the door. Only one step was separating him from her. He took a breath and opened the door...

Comments

Content
Story carries on from prompt sentence.

Organisation and cohesion
Story effectively organised.

Range
Wide range of structure and vocabulary.

Accuracy
Minimal errors.

Appropriacy of register and format
Consistently appropriate to the task.

Target reader
Would be able to follow the storyline.

Band: 5

Marks and results

Sample D (Test 3, Question 2 – Review)

> I suggested that we go out to a lovely restaurant called Kabuki's. It's a Chinese restaurant with a nice atmosphere, good food and it is a realy fun place to go at.
>
> Kabuki's has a different way making their food. You order what you want to eat and then you sit at a table that has a stove, a grill and all the equiptment. They make the food in front of you and also play games like tossing the food up in the air and you catch it with your mouth and eat it, the food is lovely and it is realy not expensive at all. The atmosphere is fun and relaxing, and suitable for everybody. It also has clean bathrooms and the staf are realy kind and entairtaining.
>
> That's why I suggested we go out to eat to Kabuki's because it is cheap, and fun and has realy tasty food. It is defently suiable for our class to go at.

Comments

Content
Good realisation of the task.

Organisation and cohesion
Ideas clearly organised.

Range
An adequate range of structure with a good range of vocabulary.

Accuracy
Generally accurate.

Appropriacy of register and format
Appropriate to the task set.

Target reader
Would be informed

Band: 4

Sample E (Test 4, Question 3 – Letter of application)

> Dear Mr James Careton,
>
> I am writing in response to your advertisement which is about the Holiday Hire Shop on the beach.
>
> First of all I think that I am the right person for this job an I am very outgoing, sociable and of course I make friends all the time because I am keen on meeting new people. In addition, I lore doing different kinds of sports and I am both a swimmer and a cyclist so I know a lot about them.
>
> As for the equipment, I have worked for three months in a shop like yours so an I have former experience on the subject, I can give useful advise to the customers, increasing the reputation of the shop. So the shop will be come more popular to teenagers.
>
> I believe that I have the right qualification for this job so I think you should hire me I am looking forward to receiving a letter from you.
>
> Yours sincerely
>
> Lydia Zitsiou

Comments

Content
Good realisation of the task.

Organisation and cohesion
Ideas clearly organised with a good range of linking devices.

Range
A good range of structure and vocabulary.

Accuracy
Generally accurate although there were some non-impeding errors.

Appropriacy of register and format
Appropriate to the task set.

Target reader
Would be informed.

Band: 4

Marks and results

Paper 3 Use of English

One mark is given for each correct answer in **Parts 1, 2** and **3**. For **Part 4**, candidates are awarded a mark of 2, 1 or 0 for each question according to the accuracy of their response. Correct spelling is required in **Parts 2, 3** and **4**. The total mark is subsequently weighted to 40.

Paper 4 Listening

One mark is given for each correct answer. The total is weighted to give a mark out of 40 for the paper. In **Part 2**, minor spelling errors are allowed, provided that the candidate's intention is clear.

For security reasons, several versions of the Listening paper are used at each administration of the examination. Before grading, the performance of the candidates in each of the versions is compared and marks adjusted to compensate for any imbalance in levels of difficulty.

Paper 5 Speaking

Candidates are assessed on their own individual performance and not in relation to each other, according to the following four analytical criteria: grammar and vocabulary, discourse management, pronunciation, and interactive communication. Assessment is based on performance in the whole test and not in particular parts of the test.

Both examiners assess the candidates. The assessor applies detailed, analytical scales, and the interlocutor applies a global achievement scale, which is based on the analytical scales.

Analytical scores

Grammar and vocabulary

This refers to the accurate and appropriate use of a range of grammatical forms and vocabulary. Performance is viewed in terms of the overall effectiveness of the language used in spoken interaction.

Discourse management

This refers to the candidate's ability to link utterances together to form coherent speech, without undue hesitation. The utterances should be relevant to the tasks and should be arranged logically to develop the themes or arguments required by the tasks.

Pronunciation

This refers to the candidate's ability to produce intelligible utterances to fulfil the task requirements. This includes stress and intonation as well as individual sounds. Examiners put themselves in the position of the non-ESOL specialist and assess the overall impact of the pronunciation and the degree of effort required to understand the candidate.

Interactive communication

This refers to the candidate's ability to take an active part in the development of the discourse. This requires the ability to participate in the range of interactive situations in the test and to develop discussions on a range of topics by initiating and responding appropriately. This also refers to the deployment of strategies to maintain interaction at an appropriate level throughout the test so that the tasks can be fulfilled.

Global achievement

This refers to the candidate's overall effectiveness in dealing with the tasks in the four separate parts of the FCE Speaking test. The global mark is an independent, impression mark which reflects the assessment of the candidate's performance from the interlocutor's perspective.

Marks

Marks for each of the criteria are awarded out of a nine-point scale. Marks for the Speaking test are subsequently weighted to produce a final mark out of 40.

FCE typical minimum adequate performance

Although there are some inaccuracies, grammar and vocabulary are sufficiently accurate in dealing with the tasks. The language is mostly coherent, with some extended discourse. Candidates can generally be understood. They are able to maintain the interaction and deal with the tasks without major prompting.

Test 1 Key

Paper 1 Reading (1 hour)

Part 1
1 D   2 C   3 A   4 B   5 D   6 A   7 B   8 C

Part 2
9 F   10 C   11 G   12 A   13 H   14 E   15 B

Part 3
16 B   17 A   18 D   19 C   20 C   21 D   22 C   23 C
24 A   25 C   26 B   27 A   28 D   29 B   30 A

Paper 2 Writing (1 hour 20 minutes)

Task-specific Mark Schemes

Part 1

Question 1

Content
The letter must include all the points in the notes:
1) make positive comment about Science Festival and/or visit
2) say which talk is preferred and why (accept no preference with reason)
3) ask Chris something else about the festival/visit
4) explain why writer is unable to stay longer.

Organisation and cohesion
Clear organisation of ideas, with suitable paragraphing, linking and opening and closing formulae as appropriate to the task.

Range
Language relating to the functions above.
Vocabulary relating to task.

Appropriacy of register and format
Consistent register and format appropriate to the situation and target reader, observing grammar and spelling conventions.

Target reader
Would be informed.

Part 2

Question 2

Content
Article should explain how the writer makes friends and give opinion as to whether friends need to agree on everything.

Organisation and cohesion
Clear organisation of ideas, with suitable paragraphing and linking.

Range
Language of explaining, describing and giving opinion.

Appropriacy of register and format
Consistent register suitable to the situation and target reader.

Target reader
Would be informed.

Question 3

Content
Story should continue from prompt sentence.

Organisation and cohesion
Storyline should be clear. Paragraphing could be minimal.

Range
Narrative tenses.
Vocabulary appropriate to the chosen topic of story.

Appropriacy of register and format
Consistent register appropriate to the story.

Target reader
Would be able to follow the storyline.

Question 4

Content
Review should give reader a clear impression of a thriller and say why people would enjoy it.

Organisation and cohesion
Clear organisation of ideas, with suitable paragraphing and linking.

Range
Language of describing, explaining and giving opinion.

Appropriacy of register and format
Consistent register suitable to the situation and target reader.

Target reader
Would be informed.

Test 1 Key

Question 5a

Content
Essay should explain who the Phantom of the Opera was and give information about past life.

Organisation and cohesion
Clear organisation of ideas, with suitable paragraphing and linking.

Range
Language of describing, explaining and expressing opinion.
Vocabulary relating to story and characters.

Appropriacy of register and format
Consistent register suitable to the situation and target reader.

Target reader
Would be informed.

Question 5b

Content
Article should describe Miss Havisham and explain why she is strange.

Organisation and cohesion
Clear organisation of ideas, with suitable paragraphing and linking.

Range
Language of describing, explaining and expressing opinion.
Vocabulary relating to story and characters.

Appropriacy of register and format
Consistent register suitable to the situation and target reader.

Target reader
Would be informed.

Paper 3   Use of English (45 minutes)

Part 1

1 B   2 D   3 A   4 C   5 B   6 A   7 C   8 D   9 D
10 C   11 C   12 B

Part 2

13 When / Whenever / As   14 only   15 which   16 be   17 long
18 whether / if   19 is   20 take   21 from   22 any   23 might / may / could
24 other

Part 3

25 popularity   26 occupations   27 extraordinarily   28 photographers
29 scenery   30 powerful   31 spectacular   32 encouraged   33 suitable
34 energetic

Part 4

35 n't/not **high** | enough (for me)   36 warmer **than** | it used to
37 a **lot** of | difference between   38 **long** as | there isn't / is not
39 **wish** (that) I | had/'d gone/been   40 **such** a | success / successful one
41 **result** of | the train('s) being/running/arriving   42 was **found** | guilty of

Paper 4 Listening (approximately 40 minutes)

Part 1

1 B   2 C   3 C   4 C   5 A   6 C   7 C   8 B

Part 2

9 weekend   10 water taxi   11 (noisy) car park / parking(-)lot   12 (evening) market
13 motorbike / motor cycle   14 mountains   15 colours   16 diving
17 simple (and) fresh   18 marmalade

Part 3

19 D   20 A   21 F   22 E   23 C

Part 4

24 B   25 C   26 B   27 C   28 A   29 C   30 A

Transcript   *This is the Cambridge First Certificate in English Listening Test. Test One.*

I am going to give you the instructions for this test. I shall introduce each part of the test and give you time to look at the questions. At the start of each piece you will hear this sound:

tone

You will hear each piece twice.

Remember, while you are listening, write your answers on the question paper. You will have five minutes at the end of the test to copy your answers onto the separate answer sheet.

There will now be a pause. Please ask any questions now, because you must not speak during the test.

[pause]

Now open your question paper and look at Part One.

[pause]

Test 1 Key

PART 1   You will hear people talking in eight different situations. For questions 1 to 8, choose the best answer, A, B or C.

Question 1   One.
You hear a woman talking on the radio about a trip to a rock festival.
Why was she at the rock festival?
A to surprise her friends
B to spend time with her son
C to keep an eye on her son

[pause]

tone

You might well ask what a mother of three was doing in a mud-drenched field with just her fourteen-year-old son, a sleeping bag and fifty-five thousand rock fans. My friends certainly did. Basically, we had decided to get rid of the family holiday and do things individually, on a one-to-one basis with each of our boys – be with them and give them lots of attention. Family holidays are all very well if you get on, but my three sons seem to have spent most of the last few years fighting each other, which is not exactly the right atmosphere for a nice, relaxing break.

[pause]

tone

[The recording is repeated.]

[pause]

Question 2   Two.
You overhear a man and a woman talking about the woman's first week in a new job.
What does she say about it?
A It was frightening.
B It was boring.
C It was tiring.

[pause]

tone

Man: You've just finished your first week nursing, haven't you? What was it like?
Woman: Not quite what I expected. I knew it would be hard work and it would leave me with little energy for other things but I was surprised how interesting it was and there is so much to learn.
Man: What were the patients like?
Woman: They seemed to be all right. I thought I'd have problems in the first few days – you hear quite scary stories about people getting things wrong, patients complaining, tough bosses. But in fact, when you're working so hard, you don't worry about things like that, you just get on with the job.

[pause]

Test 1 Key

tone

[The recording is repeated.]

[pause]

Question 3

Three.
On the radio, you hear a review of a new travel book.
What is the reviewer's opinion of the book?
A It is generally rather disappointing.
B It is a surprisingly detailed account.
C It relies too heavily on written descriptions.

[pause]

tone

Having broadcast an interview with Martin Eaves at the end of last year, we knew what to expect from this book and we've been eagerly awaiting its release. Now we've got our hands on a copy, and it hasn't disappointed. Intrigued by tales of the Vazimba people – a mysterious tribe in Madagascar, Martin packs his bags and sets off to search out the truth. *Madagascan Journey* is a fascinating mix of historical detail, adventure and humour. My only reservation concerns the illustrations. The map is sketchy to say the least and, much as I enjoyed the descriptive passages, a few more photos to help me visualise the place would have been welcome.

[pause]

tone

[The recording is repeated.]

[pause]

Question 4

Four.
You hear a journalist talking about an athlete called Helen Wright.
What is the journalist's main point?
A Helen lacks the will to win.
B Helen has always shown a natural talent.
C Helen is beginning to take running more seriously.

[pause]

tone

Speak to most athletes and they'll tell you how they ran before they could walk and how, by the third year of secondary school, there was no one anywhere near them when they were crossing the finishing line. But Helen never bothered much with running at primary school, and only joined a running club to keep a friend company, and she wasn't the fastest then. Helen didn't win anything last year either, but she isn't complaining as she came away with a bronze medal in the regional championships. She's certainly putting her athletics higher up her list of priorities these days.

121

Test 1 Key

[pause]

tone

[The recording is repeated.]

[pause]

Question 5

Five.
You overhear a man and a woman talking about holidays.
How did the woman feel about her holiday on a cruise ship?
A She regretted that the stops had been so short.
B She thought the accommodation was inadequate.
C She found the other passengers uninteresting.

[pause]

tone

Man: Where did you go on holiday last year?
Woman: We did a cruise around the Mediterranean.
Man: I went on one once, but I didn't feel comfortable. The cabins were so small. I felt I was trapped.
Woman: Well, we had lots of opportunities to go ashore to explore, although I would've preferred it if we'd had longer in port for more sightseeing.
Man: That's the bit I enjoyed most, being able to get away from the other passengers.
Woman: Actually, that wasn't a problem. I'd expected them to be older than me but that wasn't the case.

[pause]

tone

[The recording is repeated.]

[pause]

Question 6

Six.
You turn on the radio and hear a man talking about modern life.
What point is the man making about life today?
A People are lucky to be given a number of choices.
B People need to concentrate on improving their lifestyle.
C People often find life can get too complicated.

[pause]

tone

Let me give you an example of what seems to be happening more and more these days. Suppose you learn of two jobs, one with modest pay but good career prospects and another offering a high salary but fewer prospects. You make your decision, only to be lucky enough to be offered a third job in an office near the sea. Suddenly, you are given the opportunity to improve the environment you live and work in, so as a result you are left feeling confused and wondering how best to get that perfect job and lifestyle.

Test 1 Key

[pause]

tone

[The recording is repeated.]

[pause]

Question 7

Seven.
You hear a writer talking on the radio.
What is she explaining?
A why she writes about the past
B how her style of writing has changed
C where her inspiration comes from

[pause]

tone

Ever since I was a little girl in India, I've been prompted by events and my emotions to pick up the pen. Back then, I wrote poems, short stories and songs. I have a very vivid imagination. As far back as I can remember, I wrote. In India, when I wrote stories, my teacher used to read them out to the class. But even then, I didn't see this as creative, as no one used that term. I just felt that, since my teacher took the time to read my stories out to the class, they must have been OK.

[pause]

tone

[The recording is repeated.]

[pause]

Question 8

Eight.
You overhear a conversation between two teachers.
What are they planning?
A an educational trip
B a sports event
C a musical event

[pause]

tone

Woman: We've left it a bit late this year – we must get on with sorting out the details.
Man: Yes. There's a lot to do – get the players up to fitness, invite the parents, print the list of competitors. So, we need to set a date. There's a school trip, isn't there, around that time? We must make sure we don't clash with that.
Woman: No, that's sorted. They're off to Scotland the last week of March. So, as long as we avoid the school's music week at the beginning of the month, we're all right – the kids should all be free to take part.

[pause]

tone

Test 1 Key

[The recording is repeated.]

[pause]

That is the end of Part One.

Now turn to Part Two.

[pause]

PART 2 *On a travel programme, you will hear a man, Jeremy Clark, reporting from Mapé, a tropical island where people go on holiday. For questions 9 to 18, complete the sentences.*

You now have forty-five seconds to look at Part Two.

[pause]

tone

Interviewer: Our reporter, Jeremy Clark, has been on the move again. We caught up with him under the palm trees on the tropical island called Mapé. He's sent us this report.

Jeremy: If you're thinking of having *the* holiday of a lifetime then I recommend coming here. To appreciate it fully, you need a week or a fortnight, preferably a month. But even after only a weekend, I can't see myself ever wanting to go home. It really is beautiful. Mapé has no airport though, and international flights arrive on a larger island nearby. You then take what's known as a water taxi to get to Mapé. That adds about another hour on to your journey time, and if there are delays, it can be even longer. There is a helicopter service, but it's expensive and so it isn't included in the price of most holidays to the island.

My hotel, The Palm Beach, is as good as its name. Step outside and you're on the beach. Take a few more steps and you're in the water. What more could anyone wish for? Well, if it's perfection you're after then I suppose you could ask for the car park to be moved a bit further away from the other side of the hotel. If you've got a room on that side, it can be a bit noisy at times.

Another good thing about the position of the hotel is that you can easily drive into Port Mapé, the main town, if you want a change. We're not talking bright city lights and discos here – just a small town with a limited number of shops, but it has a great evening market, which is the highlight of any visit – full of people, very cheap things to buy and lots going on – more like a street theatre in some ways.

The scenery and the driving are spectacular. I hired a motorbike one day and drove around. Cars and jeeps are also available. For some reason, however, everyone tends to drive down the middle of the road whichever way they're going, so you never know what you might meet coming round a corner – very bad for the nerves. And at the northern end of the island, unlike my end, there are mountains, which are lovely, but some very frightening twisty roads. I tell you, I was glad to get back to the peace and quiet of my beach.

And talking about the beach, you know when you look at a holiday brochure and see pictures of idyllic-looking places and you think nothing can really be as good as that? Well let me tell you, it is! There are palm trees at the back for a bit of shade when it all gets too hot, but watch out for falling coconuts! And then there's the white sand and an absolutely clear blue sea. And if you're interested in wildlife, you can see all sorts of seabirds of all shapes and sizes. And the fish are really spectacular. I've never seen such incredible colours! You don't even need a mask or anything – you can just stand there in the shallow water and watch them at your feet.

There are no water sports at the hotel, but if you walk round the headland to the next bay, you'll find diving or windsurfing are on offer. There's not a huge variety, because water-skiing and power boats are both prohibited on the island, and the conditions are not right for sailing.

And finally, the food in the hotel restaurant: simple, fresh and, as far as I can see, most of it's local, from the island. We have lots of seafood and fruit. Don't ask me what it is – most of it is new to me. I thought my local supermarket in London sold a wide variety of stuff, but it's nothing compared to what you get here. It's true that some things like chocolate and ice cream are rather expensive here, but the only thing you *can't* get for some reason is marmalade. Anyway, I'm not complaining, unlike some people. The couple on the next table to mine haven't got used to the laid-back way of doing things here. It's true that the waiters in the restaurant are quite slow, but who cares, what's the hurry? Give these holidaymakers a few more days in paradise, and I'm sure they'll calm down – it's that sort of place.

[pause]

Now you will hear Part Two again.

tone

[The recording is repeated.]

[pause]

That is the end of Part Two.

Now turn to Part Three.

[pause]

PART 3

You will hear five different people talking about their work in art and design. For questions 19 to 23, choose from the list A to F what each speaker says. Use the letters only once. There is one extra letter which you do not need to use.

You now have thirty seconds to look at Part Three.

[pause]

tone

Test 1 Key

Speaker 1

As a child I used to watch my mother adjust her hat in the mirror – that's when I became fascinated with hats. I could always make things easily, even then, and now I love working the materials with my hands when I'm designing, rather than using machines. The details of the style are everything. Although I have fifteen people working in the studio, I personally design every hat, after consulting with the customer, because it's my touch they are paying for. Sometimes when I'm with one of the big designers, I think, 'Am I really here, sharing ideas with someone I used to read about in magazines?'

[pause]

Speaker 2

My work comes from my personal experiences, things that I see. Because I work in photography, there'll often be three months' preparation between having an idea and the end result. Some gallery owners don't appreciate how long it takes to perfect a photographic exhibition – so that it creates just the right effect. Now I'm being offered some great opportunities and my reaction is to say yes to everything I'm offered. But I mustn't be unrealistic and overdo it, otherwise my work won't be the same quality. There are so many new designers around, I can't afford to have a bad day. They'd be quick to step in if I did!

[pause]

Speaker 3

I spent years doing ceramics, then I met a sculptor who took me on. He never paid me, but I learnt so much – I went on from there. When I had a sculpture accepted for an exhibition, I realised that sculpting could earn me a living. Now I sell about fifteen sculptures a year, mainly through personal contacts. You never stop learning. I'm always looking for new textures and shapes. I tried working with marble this year. It took me over three months to complete the piece, so it wasn't very cost effective. But the end result was amazing, considering I'd never tackled anything like that before.

[pause]

Speaker 4

I've always been fascinated by shoes, ever since I saw them being made by hand as a child. Then I met a shoe designer at art college and it all fell into place. I feel it's important for shoes to be not only beautiful but also comfortable. You have to think of the purpose of the design, the lifestyle of the wearer – that's why it takes so long to complete. When clients come to me and say they can't walk in shoes they bought from the top designers, I know I can do better! There are so many new materials now, but you can't beat a good-quality leather, and the cut makes all the difference.

[pause]

Speaker 5

I've always had a gift for art, and so I trained as an Art teacher. Later I moved to Italy and I've been running painting holidays for fifteen years. It's a thrill working with other people's creativity. Many of the people have never painted before – they're not going to do a masterpiece in their first go, but there's so much talent around. I'm amazed at the kind of work they go on to produce. I still accept commissions, but it takes me a long time to produce a good painting. I'm not really conscious of the practicalities of being a commercial artist, I just love painting.

[pause]

Now you will hear Part Three again.

tone

[The recording is repeated.]

[pause]

That is the end of Part Three.

Now turn to Part Four.

[pause]

PART 4

You will hear a radio interview with a woman called Ivana Thomas, whose father wrote natural history articles for newspapers and magazines. For questions 24 to 30, choose the best answer, A, B or C.

You now have one minute to look at Part Four.

[pause]

tone

Interviewer: Good morning, Ivana. Welcome. We all know the articles you write in our daily newspapers, but most of us don't realise that you're doing the same job as your father did.

Ivana: Yes, my father wrote about natural history every week for forty years in a national newspaper. Half a century ago, the newspaper decided that a regular article on natural history might appeal to its readers and it came at just the right time for my father. I had just been born, his third child, and he needed to increase his income. He already wrote the occasional article for another London newspaper, but a new weekly article in a widely read daily newspaper was very welcome.

Interviewer: But he also had a full-time job, didn't he?

Ivana: Yes, he did his writing in the evenings. During the day, he worked at the Natural History Museum doing research into the octopus. Only looking at one kind of sea creature was a very narrow field and he spent hours peering down a microscope in a laboratory to study the tiniest details. Although he would never have chosen to do anything else, it was, in a way, frustrating for him because there was so much more to natural history.

Interviewer: And in his spare time?
Ivana: He continued to read widely about all the natural creatures and plants which interested him, so the articles really became part of his hobby. He used to come home from the museum and then start writing them. It was sometimes difficult for him to find a subject because, at that time, we lived on the outskirts of London, which wasn't really full of wildlife. So at the weekends, the whole family used to go on long bus rides to places like lakes and woods to look at plants and other wildlife.

Interviewer: Why didn't you move to the countryside?
Ivana: I have wondered that, but I suppose it would have been inconvenient in other ways. My father always said that the most familiar animals and birds were often the most exciting, if you took the time to sit and watch them. So he'd encourage us to take our sketchbooks, but never our cameras. He never told us to search for things which were rare or special to draw, but to enjoy what was there in front of us. I can still remember nearly all the birds and animals whose names I learnt without ever having written them down, and I've still got some of the sketches I did.

Interviewer: We know what career you've gone into, but what about your brothers? You have two, don't you?
Ivana: Yes, I do. Well, when you grow up with a parent who is so devoted to a career, the children usually either follow suit or do something completely different. Although we all did well at school in a range of subjects, both my brothers ended up working with wildlife. They've never had other ambitions in life. At the age of six, I did briefly want to be a ballet dancer, but then I was given a book about butterflies and immediately gave up the idea. I don't remember being put under pressure to follow our father – it just seemed the obvious thing to do . . . we didn't really question it.

Interviewer: And your father continued writing for the rest of his life, didn't he?
Ivana: He wrote over two thousand nature articles for the newspaper over forty years, as far as I know never missing a week. As he became less active and could no longer go out looking for subjects, he started to select particular letters from readers asking him things, and wrote about them instead.

Interviewer: And what was your father really like? What are your memories of him?
Ivana: Wherever he was, he always found something to interest him; he could never walk past something without having a look. He had great enthusiasm about his subject and through his writing he was able to communicate to others his fascination with the natural world. And he was never really aware of how successful he was – how many people read his articles and knew his name. He was just doing what he loved. He would still have done it even if nobody had paid him to.

Interviewer: And we wish you all the best, following in his footsteps.
Ivana: Thank you.

[pause]

Test 1 Key

Now you will hear Part Four again.

tone

[The recording is repeated.]

[pause]

That is the end of Part Four.

There will now be a pause of five minutes for you to copy your answers onto the separate answer sheet. Be sure to follow the numbering of all the questions. I shall remind you when there is one minute left, so that you are sure to finish in time.

[Teacher, pause the recording here for five minutes. Remind your students when they have one minute left.]

That is the end of the test. Please stop now. Your supervisor will now collect all the question papers and answer sheets.

Test 2 Key

Paper 1 Reading (1 hour)

Part 1

1 C   2 B   3 D   4 C   5 B   6 A   7 D   8 C

Part 2

9 D   10 H   11 B   12 G   13 A   14 F   15 C

Part 3

16 D   17 E   18 C   19 D   20 A   21 E   22 B   23 D
24 A   25 E   26 B   27 D   28 D   29 E   30 C

Paper 2 Writing (1 hour 20 minutes)

Task-specific Mark Schemes

Part 1

Question 1

Content
Email must include all the points in the notes:
1) tell Alex best time for visit
2) say which form of transport would be better and why (accept no preference with reason)
3) say why there will be enough to do
4) ask Alex about something else.

Organisation and cohesion
Clear organisation of ideas, with suitable paragraphing, linking and opening and closing formulae as appropriate to the task.

Range
Language relating to the functions above.
Vocabulary relating to task.

Appropriacy of register and format
Consistent register and format appropriate to the situation and target reader, observing grammar and spelling conventions.

Target reader
Would be informed.

Part 2

Question 2

Content
Article should explain which invention has changed life the most and explain why.

Organisation and cohesion
Clear organisation of ideas with suitable paragraphing and linking.

Range
Language of describing, explaining and giving opinion.

Appropriacy of register and format
Consistent register suitable to the situation and target reader.

Target reader
Would be informed.

Question 3

Content
Story should continue from prompt sentence.

Organisation and cohesion
Storyline should be clear. Paragraphing could be minimal.

Range
Narrative tenses.
Vocabulary appropriate to the chosen topic of story.

Appropriacy of register and format
Consistent register appropriate to the story.

Target reader
Would be able to follow the storyline.

Question 4

Content
Letter should include information about the candidate, which job he/she would like, and why he/she would be suitable (accept more than one job as suitable).

Organisation and cohesion
Clear organisation of ideas, with suitable paragraphing, linking and opening and closing formulae.

Range
Language of describing and explaining.
Vocabulary relating to work and skills.

Appropriacy of register and format
Consistent register suitable to the situation and target reader.

Target reader
Would be informed.

Test 2 Key

Question 5a

Content
Letter should say whether or not candidate feels sorry for Erik.

Organisation and cohesion
Clear organisation of ideas, with suitable paragraphing and linking.

Range
Language of describing, explaining and expressing opinion.
Vocabulary relating to story and characters.

Appropriacy of register and format
Consistent register suitable to the situation and target reader.

Target reader
Would be informed.

Question 5b

Content
Essay should describe Pip's 'Great Expectations' and give opinion whether he got what he expected at the end of the book.

Organisation and cohesion
Clear organisation of ideas, with suitable paragraphing and linking.

Range
Language of describing, explaining and expressing opinion.
Vocabulary relating to story and characters.

Appropriacy of register and format
Consistent register suitable to the situation and target reader.

Target reader
Would be informed.

Paper 3 Use of English (45 minutes)

Part 1

1 A   2 B   3 B   4 A   5 C   6 D   7 B   8 A   9 C
10 D   11 A   12 C

Part 2

13 for   14 which   15 if / when / once   16 in   17 were   18 few
19 Every / Each   20 with   21 A / One   22 so   23 take   24 to

Part 3

25 various   26 successful   27 encourage   28 payment   29 automatically
30 disadvantage   31 unusual   32 operation   33 popularity   34 solution

Part 4

35 German **better** | than I   36 are made / happen / occur | **because** of
37 never **had** | my car   38 was | thirty/30 years ago **that**
39 aren't / are not | **as** many   40 **took** up (playing) golf | at
41 **accused** Pierre of | leaving / having left   42 as **far** as | we could

Paper 4   Listening (approximately 40 minutes)

Part 1

1 A   2 A   3 C   4 A   5 B   6 B   7 C   8 B

Part 2

9 eight/8 months   10 Alaska   11 wool   12 white
13 sense/power of smell   14 ½/half/50% / 300 kg / three hundred kg
15 (more) vitamins   16 April   17 tent   18 (autumn) (science) lectures

Part 3

19 D   20 F   21 E   22 B   23 A

Part 4

24 B   25 B   26 C   27 C   28 A   29 B   30 C

Transcript *This is the Cambridge First Certificate in English Listening Test. Test Two.*

I am going to give you the instructions for this test. I shall introduce each part of the test and give you time to look at the questions. At the start of each piece you will hear this sound:

tone

You will hear each piece twice.

Remember, while you are listening, write your answers on the question paper. You will have five minutes at the end of the test to copy your answers onto the separate answer sheet.

There will now be a pause. Please ask any questions now, because you must not speak during the test.

[pause]

Now open your question paper and look at Part One.

[pause]

Test 2 Key

PART 1   *You will hear people talking in eight different situations. For questions 1 to 8, choose the best answer, A, B or C.*

Question 1   One.
*You hear a student talking about a school magazine he publishes.
What does he need at the moment?
A   more help
B   more articles
C   more funds*

[pause]

tone

This magazine was an ambitious project from the start. It was very different from other school magazines. I started it off with a classmate, and we had very little money – in fact my mother donated a few pounds to cover some of the initial expenses. The first issue had articles written by local politicians and even interviews with celebrities. It was a success, and lots of people outside the school bought a copy. Even if the next issue doesn't make as much, that isn't a worry. However, we're finding it difficult on our own. It's time to think of getting someone else in to lend a hand. Fortunately, there's no lack of material for future issues!

[pause]

tone

[The recording is repeated.]

[pause]

Question 2   Two.
*You hear a British woman talking about naming children.
What is her opinion on naming children?
A   She likes to avoid the most common names.
B   She thinks names will become more and more strange.
C   She is in favour of creating completely new names.*

[pause]

tone

With my own children, I wanted to choose original names, but I think some parents take it too far and make names up. I wouldn't do that. I think that's really unnatural. And I'd certainly never name a child after a famous footballer! There are parents who like to give their children really unusual names. I feel sorry for the children who have to live with those names. But then there's the other extreme, where some names are too ordinary. Anyway, in the future I think there may well be a change, with a return to more traditional names.

[pause]

tone

[The recording is repeated.]

[pause]

Question 3

Three.
You hear a man being interviewed on the radio.
What is his current occupation?
A a reporter
B a critic
C an author

[pause]

tone

Man: My wife's the one who gives me advice. She's a TV documentary presenter and listens to some of my lectures on literature and she tells me if she doesn't like it. She helps with all my projects, including my latest novel.
Woman: What's it about?
Man: Being a journalist. It's taken from when I was working for a newspaper. I loved doing that – I've based the plot on some of my experiences in that job. It's in my head all the time . . . but I sometimes think I'll never finish it.

[pause]

tone

[The recording is repeated.]

[pause]

Question 4

Four.
You hear an athlete talking about some Olympic trials he took part in.
How does he feel about his performance?
A He realises that he did not concentrate enough.
B He accepts that he had no chance against top athletes.
C He regrets that he was not in better physical condition.

[pause]

tone

I was selected for the Olympic trials and I should have got through. I thought I was stretching myself to the limit, but I just didn't do well enough. I suppose my mind was on other things. I'd just started a new job and had been putting a lot of effort into finding a place to live. All the same, I was in pretty good shape after months of training. But, you know, I'm still young and I'm sure there'll be further opportunities. Anyway, it was a great experience to line up alongside all those top athletes, and I wouldn't have wanted to miss out on that.

Test 2 Key

[pause]

tone

[The recording is repeated.]

[pause]

Question 5

Five.
You overhear two friends talking about music.
How did the man first find out about his new CD?
A He read about it.
B He heard part of it.
C He was told about it.

[pause]

tone

Man: I've just been listening to a new CD I've bought. It's a really cool new jazz album.
Woman: I didn't know you liked jazz. Did Frank tell you about it?
Man: Frank? Oh, Joanna's friend. Yeah, he's good at recommending new stuff, isn't he? But actually, they featured a track on a music programme I was listening to last week, and I went straight out to buy a copy.
Woman: I usually get useful information from the CD section in *New Music* – you know, that weekly magazine?
Man: Yes, me too. They've got some good stuff in that.

[pause]

tone

[The recording is repeated.]

[pause]

Question 6

Six.
You overhear a man talking about the competitions that he and his wife enter.
What did his favourite prize allow him to do?
A go on an interesting flight
B stay in a luxurious place
C own a prestigious car

[pause]

tone

As a hobby, my wife and I do competitions in newspapers – you know, you answer general knowledge questions and you get a prize if you win. We've won all sorts of things – two televisions, theatre tickets. But the one that stands out for me is the free weekend we had in a five-star hotel – it was incredible. We did have one let-down, though – last year, when we thought we'd won a luxury sports car – the sort everyone dreams of. We got all the correct answers, but for some reason, the prize went to somebody else. At the moment, I'm waiting to hear if we've won a trip in a balloon – that would be fascinating.

[pause]

tone

[The recording is repeated.]

[pause]

Question 7

Seven.
You hear a woman talking about her job, which involves inspecting mountain paths.
What aspect of the job does she sometimes find annoying?
A the work schedule
B the weather
C the walkers

[pause]

tone

I'm a mountain assessor, which means I try out the paths casual walkers and more experienced climbers will take, to see whether they're safe. Then I do daily reports on them. The job is split between two people. We work seven days on, seven days off; it's just as well, as it would be too much for just one person. As well as assessing, I often have to help people in difficulty. Last Sunday an icy blizzard blew over with zero visibility, and I found a young couple with no waterproofs, hats or gloves. It's unbelievable what some people will do!

[pause]

tone

[The recording is repeated.]

[pause]

Question 8

Eight.
On a radio programme, you hear a mother talking about her relationship with her daughter.
What is she surprised about?
A her daughter's decision to leave home
B how her daughter has been able to help her
C the way that her daughter's attitude has changed

137

Test 2 Key

[pause]

tone

Davina has her own place right now, but not so long ago she was living with me. In my heart she's always my little girl, but I am also aware that she's grown up and treat her accordingly – so I don't mind that she's moved out. We talked about it because I was feeling a bit insecure at first, and she was really supportive and made me see that you should follow your dream in life and adopt a positive attitude when things change. It's incredible actually, because these are things I felt *I'd* taught *her*, and there she was just giving me that same advice and reinforcing it back into my life.

[pause]

tone

[The recording is repeated.]

[pause]

That is the end of Part One.

Now turn to Part Two.

[pause]

PART 2

You will hear an interview with Alan Burgess, who has just returned from the Arctic where he was filming polar bears. For questions 9 to 18, complete the sentences.

You now have forty-five seconds to look at Part Two.

[pause]

tone

Interviewer: I'm delighted to welcome to the programme today Alan Burgess, one of our most famous wildlife film-makers. Welcome, Alan.
Alan: Thank you.
Interviewer: Now, you've just returned from the Arctic. What were you doing there?
Alan: I was with a team making a documentary about polar bears. It's actually the longest project I've ever been involved in – most of them only take two or three months. We spent about eight months in the Arctic in all, filming in Canada, Norway, Alaska and Russia.
Interviewer: What were the conditions like?
Alan: Well, we got quite used to working in minus thirty-five degrees centigrade, but the temperature dropped to minus fifty for over a week when we were in Alaska – I've never been so cold in my life! It was almost impossible to film in these conditions, so we packed up and went to Norway. There it was only minus twenty-five degrees centigrade, which was a big improvement.

Interviewer:	What clothes did you wear?
Alan:	Lots of them! I used to wear up to seven layers, with three hats and scarves and three lots of gloves. Surprisingly, the best material for these things turned out to be wool. The man-made materials used for modern skiing equipment are fine when you are active, but you need wool if you're standing around, which we were much of the time.
Interviewer:	Was it difficult getting close to film the polar bears?
Alan:	It wasn't too bad. We made sure that we only wore white clothing so that the bears couldn't see us against the snow and we even painted our camera equipment white. The main thing was to test the wind direction, to be certain that we kept downwind of the bears. They have an astonishingly powerful sense of smell – they could detect us from over a kilometre away.
Interviewer:	I'm ashamed to say I don't know very much about polar bears – I've only seen them in zoos. Can you tell me something about them? How big do they grow, for example?
Alan:	If it's standing upright, a male polar bear can be more than three metres tall, and they easily reach a weight of more than six hundred kilos, although in the summer, when there's less food, they can lose up to half their body weight.
Interviewer:	And what do they eat?
Alan:	Their main diet is seals, but in summer, when the snow has melted in places, we saw them eating plants, probably to get vitamins which they don't get from their normal diet of seals.
Interviewer:	Did you see any baby polar bears?
Alan:	Yes, in fact I think that's one of the happiest memories, seeing baby polar bears playing in the snow. They are actually born under the snow in December and don't see the outside world until April, when they are about four months old. We managed to film two cubs leaving the den with their mother for the first time. It was a marvellous moment.
Interviewer:	Were you ever in real danger?
Alan:	Just once, thank goodness, when we were in Canada. I was sleeping in my tent one night and I heard a noise outside. Thinking it was one of the team, I opened the zip a little way and, to my horror, I saw a polar bear's nose! Luckily it ran off when I shouted but it could easily have got into the tent. We did have an electric fence round the camp but when we checked it, it turned out that the battery was flat, so the polar bear had just climbed right over it.
Interviewer:	A lucky escape! Now, can you tell me about what you're planning to do next? Are you going somewhere warm for a change?
Alan:	No, not exactly. I shall be staying here for a while, actually. The Head of Natural Sciences at Bristol University has invited me to give some lectures. So for the next few months I shall be preparing a series of them for the autumn term. But after that, who knows?
Interviewer:	Well, good luck for the future, Alan, and thank you for coming in to talk to us today.

[pause]

Test 2 Key

Now you will hear Part Two again.

tone

[The recording is repeated.]

[pause]

That is the end of Part Two.

Now turn to Part Three.

[pause]

PART 3

You will hear five different people talking about their experiences as owners of small local shops. For questions 19 to 23, choose from the list A to F what each speaker says. Use the letters only once. There is one extra letter which you do not need to use.

You now have thirty seconds to look at Part Three.

[pause]

tone

Speaker 1

I sell all the basic stuff but I don't try to compete in price or range with the big supermarket five hundred metres down the road, though we sell many of the same things. For a while the real threat was two other small shops that opened nearby, but we soon came to an informal arrangement in order to survive. The one at the bottom of the street does the papers, the one at the top has more bread and cakes, and I do the vegetables. The shop was empty when I bought it in 2001. I fitted it out nicely and always try to keep it looking good.

[pause]

Speaker 2

I am open ten hours a day, every day. This is a small village, so I sell everything from apples to candles – pretty much everything. Two years ago, a supermarket opened nearby, but they closed down after a few months – there weren't enough customers to make it profitable. My shop is thriving and very much at the heart of the village. And I deliver things to the homes of people who can't make it in, even if it's just a packet of butter, and this is greatly appreciated by my retired customers. At times, the work is too much, though, and I'd welcome a break.

[pause]

Speaker 3

Some of the younger people who live around here work until about six, so they have to do their shopping in the evening. This used to be the only shop in the area which was open until ten p.m., so I had a very successful business. Things have changed, though, and I don't believe this shop will be operating in, say, four or five years. It's not just larger shops or supermarkets that are affecting us. There are too many small shops in this area, selling the same things at very similar prices. Everyone likes the idea of running their own shop, but they don't look at the bigger picture.

[pause]

Speaker 4

I open at nine a.m. and close at eleven p.m. It's very hard work, but there are still selling points for the small shop. If you work for someone else, there's no reward apart from pay, and when it comes to it, the owner can turn to you and say, 'You're too old.' Some people are very pessimistic about the future, and I tell them that, unlike supermarkets, we can offer customers the personal touch – they know our names and we know theirs. I am planning to extend my shop – you have to keep moving to succeed. Customers like supermarkets because they are cheaper, so we must offer something different.

[pause]

Speaker 5

I first got behind the counter of the family business in 1989, after giving up a job with a supermarket. It was a difficult time for small shops because people's lifestyles had changed so much. Few people had the time to prepare an evening meal as they used to; it was no longer about popping down to the shop to get things to make a meal. I see hope, though, in the fact that people are thinking more about what's in their food these days and where it comes from, and they know that the small shops are better able to provide that special local produce – like honey, for example.

[pause]

Now you will hear Part Three again.

tone

[The recording is repeated.]

[pause]

That is the end of Part Three.

Now turn to Part Four.

[pause]

PART 4 *You will hear an interview with the television actress Donna Denton. For questions 24 to 30, choose the best answer, A, B or C.*

You now have one minute to look at Part Four.

[pause]

tone

Interviewer: My guest today, Donna Denton, is a familiar face, having appeared in a number of highly successful television drama series. But Donna's not just an actress, she's also a talented singer and dancer. Which came first, Donna?

Donna: Dancing. When I was nine, my mum decided I needed a hobby. Some of my friends went horse-riding and I wanted to try it too, but it cost quite a bit. Nothing was said, but although my parents worked hard, there was never money to spare. So I chose to go to dancing classes across the road; two hours a week at only fifty p. an hour. I'm sure Mum was relieved.

Interviewer: But presumably the classes were OK?

Donna: The teacher was very tall and so glamorous that I hardly dared look at her. She immediately sent me right to the back of the class. I didn't mind because there I could dance away quite happily, out of sight. I didn't realise until later that that was where the worst dancers were put! But she didn't forget me and I slowly worked my way forward. It was a proud day when I eventually made it to the front row.

Interviewer: Where did the singing come in?

Donna: Mum heard about the Knightswell Stage School, where you did normal lessons in the morning and dance and drama in the afternoons. To get in, I had to perform in front of about twenty people – you know, in an audition. Some kids had learnt songs from musicals or bits from plays, but I just did one of the dance routines I'd learnt. They offered me a free place for a year, which was lucky. The fees were quite high and it gave my parents time to save up enough money to pay for the rest.

Interviewer: But it was the right thing for you?

Donna: I loved it. The only thing was that if you wanted to study there, you had to wear a special red jacket with the school badge on it, even outside the school building. I had a ten-minute walk to the bus stop and the local kids from the ordinary school used to laugh at me: I dreaded that journey. So Mum said to the headmistress, 'Donna's having a tough time travelling to school. Can't she change into her jacket when she arrives?' And although it was against the rules, they agreed.

Interviewer: And that was where you were expected to sing?

Donna: Once every term, you had to get up in front of the whole school and perform a song – my knees used to shake, I was so nervous, but it was good practice and, gradually, it built up my confidence. That was important because in the final year there was a singing competition. Most kids sang a classical piece, but at the last minute I decided to do a Frank Sinatra number from my dad's record collection. I don't think the choice of music had anything to do with it, but to everyone's amazement, I won.

Interviewer:	So you were headed for a singing career?
Donna:	Yes. After leaving school, I went on having private singing lessons and got some work as a backing vocalist. But it's hard to make your name as a jazz singer – which is what I'd set my heart on. So, like most of my school friends, I went after acting jobs on TV. I was more fortunate than most, getting parts in some good drama series, which allowed me to establish my name with the public. But I'd like to try other things now.
Interviewer:	So, what can we expect?
Donna:	Well, I've just completed a CD with a blues band – a dream come true for me. It'll be released next month. They've just asked me to sing with them on a world tour, actually. That was a lovely surprise but, sadly, I had to turn it down because I'd already agreed to do a month in a stage play in London on those dates. I thought of pulling out, but it wouldn't have been fair on the theatre. That's typical of show business – all or nothing – but I can't complain.
Interviewer:	Thank you, Donna, for talking . . .

[pause]

Now you will hear Part Four again.

tone

[The recording is repeated.]

[pause]

That is the end of Part Four.

There will now be a pause of five minutes for you to copy your answers onto the separate answer sheet. Be sure to follow the numbering of all the questions. I shall remind you when there is one minute left, so that you are sure to finish in time.

[Teacher, pause the recording here for five minutes. Remind your students when they have one minute left.]

That is the end of the test. Please stop now. Your supervisor will now collect all the question papers and answer sheets.

Test 3 Key

Paper 1 Reading (1 hour)

Part 1
1 C   2 A   3 B   4 C   5 D   6 A   7 D   8 B

Part 2
9 F   10 A   11 E   12 G   13 H   14 B   15 D

Part 3
16 C   17 A   18 D   19 A   20 B   21 D   22 D   23 A
24 D   25 B   26 B   27 B   28 D   29 C   30 B

Paper 2 Writing (1 hour 20 minutes)

Task-specific Mark Schemes

Part 1

Question 1

Content
Email must include all the points in the notes:
1) respond positively to Mrs Nolan attending the concert
2) describe the music/concert
3) suggest when/where photos could be taken
4) recommend person/people to interview and say why.

Organisation and cohesion
Clear organisation of ideas, with suitable paragraphing, linking and opening and closing formulae as appropriate to the task.

Range
Language relating to the functions above.
Vocabulary relating to task.

Appropriacy of register and format
Consistent register and format appropriate to the situation and target reader, observing grammar and spelling conventions.

Target reader
Would be informed.

Part 2

Question 2

Content
Review should give clear impression of the restaurant and say why it would be suitable for the class.

Organisation and cohesion
Clear organisation of ideas, with suitable paragraphing and linking.

Range
Language of describing, explaining and giving opinion.
Vocabulary relating to restaurants and visit.

Appropriacy of register and format
Consistent register suitable to the situation and target reader.

Target reader
Would be informed.

Question 3

Content
Story should continue from the prompt sentence.

Organisation and cohesion
Storyline should be clear. Paragraphing could be minimal.

Range
Narrative tenses.
Vocabulary appropriate to the chosen topic of story.

Appropriacy of register and format
Consistent register appropriate to the story.

Target reader
Would be able to follow the storyline.

Question 4

Content
Report should explain writer's view on ways for students to improve their English in their free time and say which way is best.

Organisation and cohesion
Clear organisation of ideas, with suitable paragraphing and linking.
Headings an advantage but not essential.

Range
Language of describing, explaining and giving opinion.
Vocabulary relating to studying English.

Appropriacy of register and format
Consistent register suitable to the situation and target reader.

Test 3 Key

Target reader
Would be informed.

Question 5a

Content
Essay should give writer's opinion on most unhappy character in *Phantom of the Opera*.

Organisation and cohesion
Clear organisation of ideas with suitable paragraphing and linking.

Range
Language of describing, explaining and giving opinion.
Vocabulary relating to character and storyline.

Appropriacy of register and format
Consistent register suitable to the situation and target reader.

Target reader
Would be informed.

Question 5b

Content
Letter should give the writer's opinion on whether Abel Magwitch was a bad man.

Organisation and cohesion
Clear organisation of ideas with suitable paragraphing and linking.

Range
Language of describing, explaining and giving opinion.
Vocabulary relating to characters and storyline.

Appropriacy of register and format
Consistent register suitable to the situation and target reader.

Target reader
Would be informed.

Paper 3   Use of English (45 minutes)

Part 1

1 A   2 B   3 D   4 B   5 C   6 A   7 B   8 D   9 B
10 A   11 D   12 C

Part 2

13 which   14 into   15 were   16 by   17 who   18 One
19 had   20 it / she   21 so   22 of   23 an (NOT the)   24 what

Part 3

25 enjoyment   26 leading   27 competitions   28 financial   29 wealthy
30 unusual   31 generally   32 significant   33 Professional   34 pleasure

Part 4

35 seen Tom/him | since his **wedding**
36 of a/the | **good** performance OR of (the) | **good** acting
37 n't/not live (very/too) | far **away**   38 be | **such** a
38 he would not / wouldn't | have **lost**   40 to **take** | the/a decision
41 **blamed** me | for the   42 **wished** (that) he had / he'd | sold

Paper 4 Listening (approximately 40 minutes)

Part 1

1 B   2 B   3 A   4 B   5 B   6 A   7 C   8 A

Part 2

9 stop   10 German (too)   11 (white) ears   12 female
13 30/thirty kg/kilos/kilograms   14 (tree) branches   15 (some/the) water
16 speed boat   17 (too/very) noisy   18 hands

Part 3

19 E   20 C   21 A   22 F   23 D

Part 4

24 B   25 C   26 A   27 C   28 B   29 C   30 B

Transcript

This is the Cambridge First Certificate in English Listening Test. Test Three.

I am going to give you the instructions for this test. I shall introduce each part of the test and give you time to look at the questions. At the start of each piece you will hear this sound:

tone

You will hear each piece twice.

Remember, while you are listening, write your answers on the question paper. You will have five minutes at the end of the test to copy your answers onto the separate answer sheet.

There will now be a pause. Please ask any questions now, because you must not speak during the test.

[pause]

Now open your question paper and look at Part One.

[pause]

Test 3 Key

PART I You will hear people talking in eight different situations. For questions 1 to 8, choose the best answer, A, B or C.

Question 1 One.
You hear a man talking about a teacher.
What did the teacher encourage him to do?
A to read more widely
B to do some acting
C to travel abroad

[pause]

tone

When I was in my last year of secondary school, in came Miss Gray, our new Literature teacher. She really made us love the subject. She'd been a teacher in Africa and in India, and she'd tell us about her classes there – fascinating. I was thinking at the time of joining the school theatre group but needed someone to say, 'Come on, you'll be good, go for it.' And that's what she did. She knew I loved reading plays, unlike some of my classmates, and I didn't need to be persuaded to read more. But she also knew that I was afraid of new challenges, and she helped me get over that.

[pause]

tone

[The recording is repeated.]

[pause]

Question 2 Two.
You overhear a woman talking on the phone about her computer.
Why is she complaining?
A The computer hasn't been repaired properly.
B A promise hasn't been kept.
C The computer hasn't been returned on time.

[pause]

tone

You *are* the manager, aren't you? . . . Well, all right, if he's out. . . . Look, your repair department took my computer away for repair yesterday . . . No, I don't know, but it was serious and the point is I would like a temporary replacement. . . . But it distinctly says here, in your brochure, in writing, that you lend one to customers if you have to take theirs away. . . . No, well I simply can't do without it for more than a couple of days. . . . Your workshop said it would be repaired next Wednesday, though I begin to wonder. . . . Well, in that case, why do you promise it? Better to say nothing!

[pause]

tone

148

Test 3 Key

Question 3

Three.
You hear two friends talking about a new sports centre.
What is the man's opinion of it?
A It offers value for money.
B It is conveniently located.
C It provides opportunities for socialising.

[pause]

tone

Woman: David! Long time, no see. What are you doing in this part of town?
Man: Melanie! Great! Yeah . . . of course, you live round here, don't you? I've just been to the new sports centre down the road. I've started going there twice a week.
Woman: Yeah . . . it looks really good, but I don't think I could afford it.
Man: Well, you can get a year's membership, and that only works out at about five pounds a week – and you can go as often as you want. They have lots of sports and a fantastic gym, and the staff are really friendly. Come along – it's a great place.

[pause]

tone

[The recording is repeated.]

[pause]

Question 4

Four.
You overhear a woman and a man talking at a railway station.
What does the woman want to do?
A change her travel arrangements
B find out appropriate information
C complain about the trip

[pause]

tone

Woman: So then I've got to get to Exeter by four in the afternoon. Is the best thing to take the ten o'clock train from here?
Man: Well, you could. It's a through train – you wouldn't have to change. But there are other possibilities if you were prepared to change, then you could leave later.
Woman: You mean change at Swindon? I got held up there last time. I was late for an appointment. I don't want that to happen again.
Man: Then the ten o'clock is your best bet. You'd have plenty of time spare and there's a restaurant on that train too.
Woman: Mmm.

149

Test 3 Key

[pause]

tone

[The recording is repeated.

[pause]

Question 5

Five.
You hear part of a lecture on the radio.
What is the lecturer doing?
A supporting an existing theory
B putting forward a theory of his own
C arguing against other scientists' theories

[pause]

tone

It's often said that prehistoric humans mastered language long before they invented music. But scientists now believe that even our most distant ancestors may have been able to sing. Indeed, it could be that singing came before language rather than the other way round. The earliest form of human sound, they suggest, could have been a type of singing, intended to express people's emotions rather than to pass on information. My research goes one step further, however, because I suspect that some of the earliest stone tools and weapons that have been discovered could actually have been primitive musical instruments, although this is something which I've found very difficult to prove.

[pause]

tone

[The recording is repeated.]

[pause]

Question 6

Six.
You overhear a woman telling a friend about something she attended recently at her local college.
What is she describing?
A a concert
B a lesson
C a talk

[pause]

tone

I thought it was a great success. He hadn't done it in front of people before except to his students so it was important it went well. Some people complained afterwards because they said they couldn't hear what he said between each piece, but others said that didn't matter. They were really impressed by the fact they were all his own compositions and the quality of the sound was superb, especially on the high notes. And they did get a chance to go up and ask him questions at the end if they wanted.

[pause]

tone

[The recording is repeated.]

[pause]

Question 7

Seven.
You overhear a man and a woman who used to study at the same school talking together.
In the man's opinion, what was the woman like at school?
A forgetful
B lazy
C untidy

[pause]

tone

Man: It's hard to believe how people can change as they get older. Look at you! You're a business executive now, responsible for a large department.
Woman: Yes. Remember what I was like at school? Always in trouble for being lazy and leaving everything to the last minute.
Man: You weren't really lazy. You just didn't work more than absolutely necessary. But you *were* messy. You drove everyone mad leaving stuff all over the place. And you seemed to be in a dream half the time, forgetting things. But I think you just pretended to be forgetful.
Woman: That's true. It was convenient sometimes.
Man: And now . . . you're a high flyer!

[pause]

tone

[The recording is repeated.]

[pause]

Question 8

Eight.
You hear a tennis player talking about how he hurt himself.
What does he think caused his injury?
A lifting something before a game
B failing to prepare himself for a game
C playing a difficult shot during a game

[pause]

tone

Well, I got to the gate at the back of the sports centre in Percy Street. It was locked, but I managed to get my bike over the fence. And that's when it must have happened – stupid really, when you think about it, but I couldn't be bothered to cycle round to the main entrance. Anyway, I got changed and Jim was waiting on the court. I did my usual bit of warming up – stretching the leg muscles and so on – but the first ball I hit, well, that was it. I felt this shooting pain right down my arm and the racket just fell out of my hand.

[pause]

tone

[The recording is repeated.]

[pause]

That is the end of Part One.

Now turn to Part Two.

[pause]

PART 2

You will hear a man called Jeremy Baker talking about different ways of travelling in northern Finland. For questions 9 to 18, complete the sentences.

You now have forty-five seconds to look at Part Two.

[pause]

tone

Interviewer: Jeremy, I know you've just come back from Finland. And you had some interesting experiences with transport while you were there, didn't you?

Jeremy: Yes, I did. I spent a week two hundred and fifty kilometres north of the Arctic Circle, where there were only a few hours of sunlight every day and the temperature was minus thirty degrees Celsius. But it was a marvellous trip!

What made it really exciting for me was the dogs. I went on a ride across the snow on a sled pulled by four dogs, or huskies as they're called. They're amazing animals and I loved getting them to obey my commands. You can shout 'left' or 'right' to them and they'll obey immediately. But what I found myself shouting more than anything was the word 'stop' – just to make sure they knew who was in control! And what was extraordinary about my huskies was that they obey these commands in more than one language. Obviously, they understand Finnish, but my guide told me they'll respond to German too. If I'd been there longer, I'd have taught them some French – just for the fun of it!

Anyway, my guide and I set off on two dog sleds into the frozen Finnish countryside. To begin with, I was too preoccupied with controlling the dogs to admire the wonderful scenery. Those huskies certainly love to run! Their tongues hang out, their noses strain forward and their tails stream behind them. I didn't take my eyes off the lead dog. It had white ears, and if I looked at them, it helped me concentrate on where we were going.

My lead dog was an exceptionally intelligent animal, though they always have to be smart. Apparently, they are also usually female. There are male dogs in the team, too, but they don't take the lead position.

As I said, my sled had four dogs, but you need eight or ten to pull a sled going with a full load of two hundred kilos. Each individual dog is capable of hauling thirty kilos, and they seem to do it almost effortlessly.

At first, we were dashing along in the open countryside, but after about an hour we turned into the forest. We disturbed a few birds, and snow would come falling down out of the trees. But branches were the things I really had to look out for. I certainly didn't want to get one in my face!

Eventually, we got to a cabin where we were going to have lunch. My guide started a fire and set about preparing a meal of reindeer meat, washed down with juice made from berries that grow in the forest. He sent me off with a bucket to fetch some water. This involved making a hole in the ice on a nearby lake. I must say, I was quite nervous that the ice was going to break underneath my weight!

That dog sled ride was the best part of my trip, but there are other exciting ways to get around on the ice and snow. Another way I tried was riding a skidoo. It's a great favourite with those of us who love racing about without much purpose, and some people compare a skidoo to a motorbike; but to my mind it feels much more like travelling on a speed boat. It's certainly faster than being pulled by dogs. But, for me, its big disadvantage is that it's very noisy. The sound of the engine destroys the peace of the countryside. But, thanks to my skidoo, I was able to travel deep into the wilderness to spend the night in a cabin by a frozen lake. I'll never forget the incredibly beautiful night sky I saw there. The advantage of skidoo-riding is that you never have icy hands, however low the temperature falls. This is thanks to the vehicle's heated handlebars. I wish there was something similar for your feet.

Interviewer: It sounds like an interesting trip. Would you go back to Finland?
Jeremy: Oh, definitely.

[pause]

Now you will hear Part Two again.

tone

[The recording is repeated.]

[pause]

That is the end of Part Two.

Now turn to Part Three.

[pause]

PART 3

You will hear five different people talking about shopping for clothes. For questions 19 to 23, choose from the list A to F what each speaker says. Use the letters only once. There is one extra letter which you do not need to use.

You now have thirty seconds to look at Part Three.

[pause]

tone

Speaker 1

I don't really do a lot of shopping – I've got more important things to do – and that's why I tend to go to a small boutique in the city centre. They sell the type of thing which suits me. I usually go if I want an outfit for a special occasion – and then I'll leave it until the last moment! I don't even try things on – the trousers, for example, I know will fit me perfectly. The price may be a bit of a shock, but it's not as if I do it every month, so I can afford it. I don't remember ever buying an item I didn't really need.

[pause]

Speaker 2

As I work in the fashion industry, you might think I'd have a wardrobe full of clothes. In fact, I'm very choosy. I'm surrounded by images of clothes all day long, so I'm able to decide what's just right for me, and we're always creating designs for the next season. So I can buy exactly what I need – I like to think I have the right thing for when the weather changes, rather than dashing into the shops at the last minute. I do spend a lot on my clothes, but I think it's worth investing in quality – the best styles don't go out of fashion.

[pause]

Speaker 3

Shopping is almost like a hobby for me, though my sister's always telling me I could be doing something more useful. I love it when winter's over and I can start buying summer clothes. I try to concentrate on the essentials, but then, like the other day, I caught sight of a dress in a shop window when I was on the bus. I jumped off and walked back to get it, and it looked great when I tried it on, but I've never actually worn it – like a lot of things in my wardrobe. My friends think I waste money, but they just don't understand.

[pause]

Speaker 4

I've lived in jeans and T-shirts for years because it's easy, but when I got this new job I realised I'd have to face up to wearing a boring shirt, collar and tie to work. I was dreading it. I thought, I'm going to have to spend all my salary increase on two new jackets – they cost a fortune! But when I got into town, a lot of the clothes shops had big reductions on everything. I never like to buy the first thing I see, though – I must have tried on about twenty jackets. I find it impossible to decide what looks best on me, so I usually rely on my girlfriend's advice.

[pause]

Speaker 5

I love looking through magazines to see all the latest fashions, but of course, the models in there are tall and slim, and with my figure I have to be very careful about what I buy. That's why, if I find a style that suits me, I sometimes buy it in several colours. My parents accuse me of being extravagant with clothes, but that's rubbish. When I get fed up with something, it's pointless keeping it; I don't like clothes that go on for years. I don't waste any time thinking about it – I sell them to a second-hand shop, which means I've got money to buy something new.

[pause]

Now you will hear Part Three again.

tone

[The recording is repeated.]

[pause]

That is the end of Part Three.

Now turn to Part Four.

[pause]

PART 4

You will hear part of an interview with the actor and film director Charles Martin. For questions 24 to 30, choose the best answer, A, B or C.

You now have one minute to look at Part Four.

[pause]

tone

Interviewer: My guest today is the actor and film director Charles Martin. Welcome, Charles. Now let's start at the beginning. You played a part in the American TV series *Cowboys* for about six years.

Charles: That's right. I never dreamed I'd work steadily for six years, and in the same part – that's unusual in the acting profession. I managed to save a little money during that time, figuring I'd maybe get to a low period without work; but as it happened, something always turned up.

Interviewer: It certainly did – you were discovered by the film-maker Mario Urresti and starred in some very popular films. What attracted you to the first one?

Charles: Well, Mario came up with this idea of reinterpreting an ancient legend and setting it in nineteenth-century Mexico, which was quite adventurous in itself, and then, because of Mario's contacts, it was easier to make the movie in Spain. My part wasn't so different from my TV work, but the film had a definite Spanish flavour, with all the local actors as well as guys from Italy – very exotic for a young American guy!

Interviewer: Now, your style of acting was very quiet, almost silent. Did people understand what you were doing?

Charles: I think the producers were concerned initially. I had this image of how my character, Miguel, should be and I persuaded them to cut a lot of dialogue from the original screenplay. In movies today there are so many close-ups that you can do a lot without having to say much, if you know what I mean, unlike the old silent movies, where actors felt obliged to overplay everything. Perhaps they figured audiences wouldn't understand unless they used exaggerated gestures and expressions.

Interviewer:	In your next big film, *The Good Cop*, you played a very angry young man. How much of that was acting?
Charles:	People suggested all sorts of reasons for my anger, which I found rather surprising. I certainly have an ability to express anger – that's part of my job. It was an exciting detective story which was making some relevant points, and it was a welcome change from what I'd been doing.
Interviewer:	Later you turned to directing. Was that something you'd wanted to do for a long time?
Charles:	Yeah, but I had to wait for the right opportunity with the film *Just for a Laugh*.
Interviewer:	You got your friend John Dawson, who'd directed you in several films, to act in *Just for a Laugh*. Was it because you were nervous about directing?
Charles:	That was what everyone said. What I felt, though, was that he'd become a better director if he had to be an actor for a change, just as I became a better actor by getting behind the camera. I used to joke with John that if I got stuck when I was telling the actors what to do, he'd be there to help out.
Interviewer:	You're said to be a very dynamic and lively director. Where does that come from?
Charles:	I do what's necessary. If it's quick, that's fine. If there are problems, then I'll stay until I get what I want. Great actors will come loaded with ideas. Part of the joy of shooting a movie is seeing how they do it. It's like conducting an orchestra. The first time you hear the music that you've just seen as notes on a page, some sections surprise you.
Interviewer:	Everyone's surprised that your movies are completed on time and within budget. How do you do it?
Charles:	I've been around a lot of movie sets as an actor where so much time was wasted from having to repeat scenes so many times. My way is everybody comes prepared, with their lines learned, and they know there'll only be one or two takes of a scene, not fifteen or twenty. That way they remember how they acted – so that leads on smoothly to the next section. That gives everyone in front of, and behind, the cameras more belief in the project. They work hard but they have more time for themselves.
Interviewer:	So, what's next . . .

[pause]

Now you will hear Part Four again.

tone

[The recording is repeated.]

[pause]

That is the end of Part Four.

There will now be a pause of five minutes for you to copy your answers onto the separate answer sheet. Be sure to follow the numbering of all the questions. I shall remind you when there is one minute left, so that you are sure to finish in time.

[Teacher, pause the recording here for five minutes. Remind your students when they have one minute left.]

That is the end of the test. Please stop now. Your supervisor will now collect all the question papers and answer sheets.

Test 4 Key

Paper 1 Reading (1 hour)

Part 1
1 D   2 C   3 C   4 B   5 D   6 B   7 A   8 C

Part 2
9 D   10 H   11 A   12 B   13 C   14 G   15 E

Part 3
16 D   17 C   18 A   19 D   20 C   21 B   22 D   23 A
24 B   25 B   26 D   27 A   28 C   29 D   30 A

Paper 2 Writing (1 hour 20 minutes)

Task-specific Mark Schemes

Part 1

Question 1

Content
Email must include all the points in the notes:
1) make a positive comment about party arrangements
2) say what should be done about food and why (acceptable to leave the choice to Anna)
3) make a suggestion about music
4) give opinion about dress (accept interpretation of 'fancy' as formal).

Organisation and cohesion
Clear organisation of ideas, with suitable paragraphing, linking and opening and closing formulae as appropriate to the task.

Range
Language relating to the functions above.
Vocabulary relating to task.

Appropriacy of register and format
Consistent register and format appropriate to the situation and target reader, observing grammar and spelling conventions.

Target reader
Would be informed.

Test 4 Key

Part 2

Question 2

Content
Essay should include reference to two subjects, explaining why they are useful for future life.

Organisation and cohesion
Clear organisation of ideas with suitable paragraphing and linking.

Range
Language of describing, explaining and giving opinion.
Vocabulary relating to subjects chosen.

Appropriacy of register and format
Consistent register suitable to the situation and target reader.

Target reader
Would be informed.

Question 3

Content
Letter should explain why writer is suitable for job. Not necessary to address all bullet points.

Organisation and cohesion
Clear organisation of ideas, with suitable paragraphing, linking and opening and closing formulae.

Range
Language of describing, explaining and giving opinion.
Vocabulary relating to holiday shop.

Appropriacy of register and format
Consistent register suitable to the situation and target reader.

Target reader
Would be informed.

Question 4

Content
Story should continue from the prompt sentence.

Organisation and cohesion
Storyline should be clear. Paragraphing could be minimal.

Range
Narrative tenses.
Vocabulary appropriate to the chosen topic of story.

Appropriacy of register and format
Consistent register appropriate to the story.

Target reader
Would be able to follow the storyline.

Question 5a

Content
Essay should explain whether money makes Pip happy.

Organisation and cohesion
Clear organisation of ideas, with suitable paragraphing and linking.

Range
Language of describing, explaining and giving opinion.
Vocabulary relating to story and characters.

Appropriacy of register and format
Consistent register suitable to the situation and target reader.

Target reader
Would be informed.

Question 5b

Content
Letter should explain why Erik allowed Christine to leave and marry Raoul.

Organisation and cohesion
Clear organisation of ideas, with suitable paragraphing and linking.

Range
Language of describing, explaining and giving opinion.
Vocabulary relating to story and characters.

Appropriacy of register and format
Consistent register suitable to the situation and target reader.

Target reader
Would be informed.

Paper 3 Use of English (45 minutes)

Part 1

1 D   2 C   3 A   4 C   5 B   6 A   7 A   8 C   9 B
10 B   11 B   12 D

Part 2

13 since   14 came   15 for   16 of / about   17 (in)to   18 what
19 was   20 so   21 this / that   22 over / through   23 to   24 a

Part 3

25 strength   26 loss   27 significant   28 decision
29 instructors (NOT instructor)   30 recommendation   31 injury
32 uncomfortable   33 gradually   34 distances

Test 4 Key

Part 4

35 I would not / wouldn't | **listen** to
36 from Naomi | **nobody** (else) is OR from Naomi | there is **nobody**
37 **how** deep | the pool   38 be | **pulled** down
39 no **doubt** | in my   40 if/whether she/he | **could** (possibly) look
41 me not | to arrive/be/come **late**   42 **made** me | lose

Paper 4   Listening (approximately 40 minutes)

Part 1

1 B   2 C   3 B   4 A   5 B   6 A   7 A   8 B

Part 2

9 snakes   10 ill / sick / unwell / not well   11 water   12 (eating) (the) grapes
13 arm   14 students   15 (a) cake / cakes   16 bus   17 biology
18 (famous) (conservation/research) (nature) park / reserve / (natural) reservation / animal/ wildlife/safari park / conservation/research area

Part 3

19 F   20 B   21 A   22 E   23 C

Part 4

24 B   25 A   26 C   27 A   28 B   29 C   30 B

Transcript   This is the Cambridge First Certificate in English Listening Test. Test Four.

I am going to give you the instructions for this test. I shall introduce each part of the test and give you time to look at the questions. At the start of each piece you will hear this sound:

tone

You will hear each piece twice.

Remember, while you are listening, write your answers on the question paper. You will have five minutes at the end of the test to copy your answers onto the separate answer sheet.

There will now be a pause. Please ask any questions now, because you must not speak during the test.

[pause]

Now open your question paper and look at Part One.

[pause]

Test 4 Key

PART 1   *You will hear people talking in eight different situations. For questions 1 to 8, choose the best answer, A, B or C.*

Question 1   One.
You hear a young fashion model talking about the first magazine feature she appeared in.
Why were she and her sister chosen for the feature?
A They were willing to change their hair colour.
B They looked very similar to each other.
C They looked good in the designer clothes.

[pause]

tone

Well, basically, what happened was they were looking for, like, a blonde girl to appear in this 'before and after' magazine feature. You know, they let a hair stylist and a make-up person loose on you and put you in designer clothes, then they publish photos to show how much better you look afterwards. Anyway, they weren't actually looking for twins, but like, our mum sent in a photo of both of us together and I guess they just thought, like, 'Hey yeah . . . that's not a bad idea, we can make them look different to each other.' Because until then, only our mum had been able to tell us apart.

[pause]

tone

[The recording is repeated.]

[pause]

Question 2   Two.
You hear a woman on the radio talking about her experiences at ballet school.
How did she feel when she left the school?
A relieved
B embarrassed
C depressed

[pause]

tone

Well, I wanted to be a dancer. And my parents supported me in my ambition, too. So at the age of fifteen, I went to ballet school. But it didn't work out, unfortunately. Schools like that want to take you apart and put you back together again. It's part of the discipline, but your character is suppressed. Anyway, I didn't stay there long – I got kicked out at the end of my first year. At the time, it was a low point for me – I considered myself a failure – but now I can see that it set me on a path to what I do now, working as a TV presenter.

[pause]

Test 4 Key

tone

[The recording is repeated.]

[pause]

Question 3   Three.
You hear a student talking about a part-time job he does.
What attracted him to this particular job?
A   the opportunities for promotion
B   the chance to use skills he already had
C   the amount of money he is able to earn

[pause]

tone

I started as a general helper at the kart-racing centre. Now I've worked my way up to race director, which I never expected. I've always been interested in cars and I know a little bit about car maintenance, so this was exactly what I had in mind when I set out to find a part-time job. It's not exactly hard work and I get to have a laugh with my mates. It's also good to get away from college work a few nights a week, and of course I earn around a hundred pounds a week. I could make more elsewhere, I know, but I wanted more from the experience than just pocket money.

[pause]

tone

[The recording is repeated.]

[pause]

Question 4   Four.
You overhear a man and a woman talking about a ride at a theme park.
What does the man say about the ride?
A   It was too short.
B   It was too expensive.
C   It was too frightening.

[pause]

tone

Woman: That was fantastic! Shall we go again?
Man: Not me. I could live without doing that again. It was over so quickly.
Woman: You were determined not to enjoy it before we got on – you moaned about the cost.
Man: No, really, it wasn't that. I just thought there'd be more to it.
Woman: Judging by the colour of your face, I reckon you were scared. You'd probably have been sick if we'd stayed on any longer.
Man: Oh yeah? Have you seen the colour of *your* face?

[pause]

162

Test 4 Key

tone

[The recording is repeated.]

[pause]

Question 5   Five.
You hear an announcement at the train station.
Who would find this announcement relevant?
A passengers waiting for the train from Wellington
B passengers waiting to board the Hamilton train
C passengers waiting on platform four

[pause]

tone

Attention, this is a platform alteration. All passengers waiting on platform five for the train to Hamilton should now go to platform four where the train is due to arrive. We regret that this train is subject to a delay of up to twenty minutes. We are very sorry for the inconvenience this may cause to your journey. The train now standing at platform eight is the eight fifteen to Wellington. Please note this is a special excursion train and is not timetabled.

[pause]

tone

[The recording is repeated.]

[pause]

Question 6   Six.
You overhear two people in a clothes shop talking about some trousers.
What do they both like?
A the style
B the colour
C the material

[pause]

tone

Woman: What do you think about these then? I like the way they do up at the back.
Man: Mmm, they suit you. Black though, not a very summery colour.
Woman: Oh I don't know – black's good any time of the year.
Man: They *look* quite thick. Are they?
Woman: Not particularly – they're linen, they feel rather cool.
Man: How much are they?
Woman: Let's see – eighty pounds – mmm . . . quite a lot for a pair of trousers I don't really need.
Man: Jenny! Why are we wasting our time if you don't need them? Let's go and have lunch instead.

[pause]

Test 4 Key

tone

[The recording is repeated.]

[pause]

Question 7   Seven.
You overhear a teacher talking to her students.
What is she doing?
A advising them of room changes
B informing them about additional classes
C explaining about new tutor group meeting times

[pause]

tone

Please look at the timetable you've just been given as there are one or two things I'd like to go over with you. This is the final one for the term and, as you can see, it doesn't include any *extra* lessons, which will be arranged with you individually as usual. So, no change there. However, please note that all the exam practice classes will be held in the new teaching block which was completed during the holidays. So you'll have to check the room numbers carefully. These changes do not affect tutor group meetings, which will be at five p.m. every day as they were last term.

[pause]

tone

[The recording is repeated.]

[pause]

Question 8   Eight.
You hear part of a radio interview with a rock musician who is performing in his home town.
What do the two speakers agree about?
A Tickets for rock concerts in the town are expensive.
B There is a lack of suitable venues in the town.
C The music scene in the town is very lively.

[pause]

tone

Interviewer: Welcome back to your home town, Rod.
Rod: Great to be here. Quite a dynamic place for music these days, isn't it?
Interviewer: It used to be more so, I think. Now, your concert's on Sunday, in Queen's Square. Tickets fifty pounds – mmm . . . that's quite a lot.
Rod: Standard price here these days, I'm told, and anyway the kids can afford it. But it's ridiculous – a town this size should have a proper arena for concerts like these.

164

Test 4 Key

Interviewer: Well, there's Colgate Hall.
Rod: Yeah, great for classical concerts where everyone's sitting quietly in their seats, but not for rock bands.
Interviewer: True, there's not much room to move around.

[pause]

tone

[The recording is repeated.]

[pause]

That is the end of Part One.

Now turn to Part Two.

[pause]

PART 2 *You will hear an interview with a man called Lucas Doran, who is talking about his job as a zookeeper. For questions 9 to 18, complete the sentences.*

You now have forty-five seconds to look at Part Two.

[pause]

tone

Interviewer: Good morning, and in the studio today we have Lucas Doran, who is in charge of what's called the Monkey House at Melchester Zoo, where not only monkeys but also the big apes, such as gorillas, are kept. Lucas, welcome. How did you get to work with gorillas?
Lucas: I've worked at the zoo for some time. I began with the snakes, which was brilliant, and then moved on to the rhinos, which wasn't quite so interesting. My ambition was always to work with big cats like lions and tigers, so when they transferred me to the Monkey House, I was disappointed at first. But later on I realised how lucky I was, because monkeys are so clever – they're always trying to trick you!
Interviewer: That must keep you on your toes! Tell us about your day.
Lucas: I get to work about seven forty-five and the first job is to look at the animals. Nobody's on duty at night, so we have to make sure none of them is ill, or whether any babies have been born; you see, most monkeys give birth at night. Then we clean the cages and change the water. Then later on in the day, we return and put down fresh straw for their bedding.
Interviewer: What about feeding the animals?
Lucas: They are fed four times a day in summer and three in winter. The monkeys eat anything really – fruit, vegetables, cooked meat, insects. But grapes are their favourite, though.

Interviewer:	Have you ever been hurt by one of the animals?
Lucas:	Once. A young female gorilla got out one day. I was just sweeping a path and I felt someone coming up behind me. I turned and there she was. I walked toward her talking calmly, and she just put a hand on my chest and pushed me out of the way. Quite gently for a gorilla, but enough to knock me off my feet. I fell over and broke my arm. Fortunately, just then her baby, which was still inside the cage, cried and she ran back inside to take care of it.
Interviewer:	Gosh, that was lucky. Now, I'd like to move on to your relationship with the public.
Lucas:	Well, I feel a big part of my job is helping people to understand about the animals. Lots of families come to the zoo at the weekend and I answer their questions. And I especially enjoy my talks with the students who come during the week. Then sometimes we have lecturers visiting, who give interesting talks.
Interviewer:	Right.
Lucas:	But what I really can't stand is when people feed the monkeys. It's not so bad if they give them fruit, because at least apples and bananas form part of their natural diet, but we do say 'please don't feed the animals', and people should know that things like cake are not good for them.
Interviewer:	Do you have any funny stories about your time here?
Lucas:	Well, one time I had to look after two newborn baby monkeys. Their mother wasn't interested in them, so I had to feed them milk from a bottle every two hours. I had to take them back to my flat in a box on the bus because my car had broken down and I couldn't find a taxi driver willing to take them. They slept most of the way, but I got some very strange looks when these hairy little fingers occasionally crept out of the box!
Interviewer:	And what of the future?
Lucas:	Well, I've recently gone back to studying. Because I'm interested in running my own zoo one day, I need to get some more qualifications. At first, I thought I needed to study Animal Psychology or Zoology, but actually the most useful course turned out to be one in Biology. I was always good at maths and sciences, so I'm really enjoying it.
Interviewer:	Right.
Lucas:	But what I'd really like to do is visit Africa. Not as a tourist on some safari, staying in the best hotels, but actually to meet the famous conservationist Briget Foley, and see the park where she does her research into apes and monkeys. It would be really exciting to see some of the animals I know so well from the zoo in their natural surroundings.
Interviewer:	Well, Lucas, best of luck with both those projects and thank you for joining us today.
Lucas:	Thank you.

[pause]

Now you will hear Part Two again.

tone

[The recording is repeated.]

[pause]

Test 4 Key

That is the end of Part Two.

Now turn to Part Three.

[pause]

PART 3

You will hear five different people talking about taking photographs. For questions 19 to 23, choose from the list A to F the subject that each person is most interested in photographing. Use the letters only once. There is one extra letter which you do not need to use.

You now have thirty seconds to look at Part Three.

[pause]

tone

Speaker 1

Being a professional photographer probably seems like a glamorous job, especially if you work for a gossip magazine and have access to fabulously rich and beautiful people. Actually, I've done society photography, and it's difficult work – fun, but limiting. I gave it up after a few years and now I work on the sports page of a national newspaper, which is OK. But what I really love doing is pictures of everyday life in my own home – meals, special events, the kids playing. I avoid the usual holiday snaps of us all lined up by a swimming pool in some resort. I leave that to other people.

[pause]

Speaker 2

I'm a professional photographer and I earn my living by doing portraits of well-known people. I absolutely love my job because I have to discover the real person behind the image, and I find the challenge fascinating. My hobby is travelling, but I leave my camera behind when I'm on holiday, to have a rest from taking photographs. But I always carry a sketchbook around with me, to draw flowers and plants. Sometimes when I see a particularly interesting face or landscape, I wish I could reach for my camera, because my drawing skills aren't up to those sorts of subjects.

[pause]

Speaker 3

I used to have a darkroom where I developed my own photos. I don't have time for that any more since I've got a young family, but I'm still interested in photography. I've bought a digital camera, which is wonderful – small and light and easy to use, and I take it with me everywhere. There's always something going on in our city, and when I'm out and about I keep my eyes open for interesting events and take photos. I've started sending pictures in to the local paper, and they're sometimes printed on the front page. The only thing I'm not keen on is sport, to my children's disappointment.

[pause]

Test 4 Key

Speaker 4

My dream was to be a photojournalist – work for a famous newspaper or magazine and travel round the world following the big news stories of the day. I did train as a photographer at college, but photojournalism is a tough area to work in, competitive and often dangerous. In the end I got a job as a photographer on a wildlife magazine, and that is completely absorbing. I drive my family mad because I have my camera with me all the time, taking pictures of anything that moves, and I sometimes feel I can only see properly through a lens.

[pause]

Speaker 5

My first job after school was on our local paper, photographing news events, like a celebrity opening a new supermarket or graduation day at a school. It was useful training for me, and when I got a job later on a national newspaper I developed an instinct for getting a good picture. I don't specialise in any particular department on the paper where I work now, but go where I'm sent. I particularly like it when I cover an athletics meeting and get a position near the finishing line, where I can catch the expressions, the extremes of emotion on people's faces as they come in.

[pause]

Now you will hear Part Three again.

tone

[The recording is repeated.]

[pause]

That is the end of Part Three.

Now turn to Part Four.

[pause]

PART 4

You will hear a radio interview with two students, Annabelle Lester and Roberto Marini, who are both studying at the same art school. For questions 24 to 30, choose the best answer, A, B or C.

You now have one minute to look at Part Four.

[pause]

tone

Interviewer:	I'm visiting the Capital Art School where I'm meeting two students, Annabelle Lester and Roberto Marini. Annabelle, what sort of course are you doing?
Annabelle:	It's a three-year Fine Art course, which covers just about everything. It's really hard work because there's so much to do in such a short time. But I'm getting a lot out of it. We don't specialise: the idea is that we learn to work with all sorts of media, from the traditional art forms like sculpture and painting, to print-making and film production. The school aims to represent the art of today, in whatever form it takes.
Interviewer:	Roberto, I can see that practical work is the most important part of the course, but do you have lectures as well?
Roberto:	Yes, and not only from our tutors. If you want to make a living as an artist, you've got to know about the different openings there are in the art world, but also about the financial side of things; so we get talks from accountants and agents, as well as art historians and people who run galleries. And sometimes professional artists come in to give lectures or do workshops with us.
Interviewer:	There's a big choice of art schools in London. Why did you choose to come here, Annabelle?
Annabelle:	Actually, the school chose me, and I was really lucky. Hundreds of people apply for a place here. One of the reasons is that the teaching is free, which means a lot when you have the expenses we do – materials, equipment and so on. But that wasn't my reason. I wanted to come here because we can experiment and be original, do anything we like; and the teaching is good – the tutors are positive and supportive about everything we do.
Interviewer:	Roberto, what are you working on at the moment?
Roberto:	The course I'm doing shows how the design of familiar things around us, like say a hairdryer, can be similar to something we think of as art, like a sculpture. I cut out illustrations from art magazines and store catalogues and stick them up all over my studio walls to give me ideas. The objective is to find inspiration for my art in the products you find in the shops.
Interviewer:	So, how exactly do you make your art?
Roberto:	Well, for the research stage, I photograph household objects with a digital camera, then change their appearance on my computer. When I'm satisfied there's enough material to work with, I make copies and finish them off by hand. They then have to go to the printers to be enlarged. We all have laptops, and our tutors email us feedback reports on what we've done for our records.
Interviewer:	Are you pleased with the technical equipment that you have here, Annabelle?
Annabelle:	Absolutely. We've got totally up-to-the-minute facilities here, because a local company has donated very sophisticated equipment to the school, and that allows us to experiment with things we couldn't afford to buy ourselves. They don't even mind if we damage it trying to do complex designs, because the idea is that art students should try out uses for the machines that no one has thought of before.

Test 4 Key

Interviewer:	I suppose then that, when you finish your course, you can go in either direction – industrial design or fine art?
Annabelle:	Yes. It'll be difficult to choose because both worlds are interesting. But I've got a long way to go yet before I can say I'm a professional artist. Standards of industrial design are tremendously high, and competition to get jobs in that field is fierce; but I'm going to try because it's even tougher to make a living from fine art, selling your work to art galleries. There's teaching, of course . . . Anyway, all of us here are absolutely committed and very, very ambitious.
Interviewer:	I'm sure both of you will do well. Thank you.

[pause]

Now you will hear Part Four again.

tone

[The recording is repeated.]

[pause]

That is the end of Part Four.

There will now be a pause of five minutes for you to copy your answers onto the separate answer sheet. Be sure to follow the numbering of all the questions. I shall remind you when there is one minute left, so that you are sure to finish in time.

[Teacher, pause the recording here for five minutes. Remind your students when they have one minute left.]

That is the end of the test. Please stop now. Your supervisor will now collect all the question papers and answer sheets.

Sample answer sheet: Paper 1

SAMPLE

UNIVERSITY of CAMBRIDGE
ESOL Examinations

Candidate Name
If not already printed, write name in CAPITALS and complete the Candidate No. grid (in pencil).

Candidate Signature

Examination Title

Centre

Supervisor:
If the candidate is ABSENT or has WITHDRAWN shade here ▭

Centre No.

Candidate No.

Examination Details

Candidate Answer Sheet

Instructions

Use a PENCIL (B or HB).

Mark ONE letter for each question.

For example, if you think B is the right answer to the question, mark your answer sheet like this:

0 A B̲ C D E F G H

Rub out any answer you wish to change using an eraser.

#	Answers	#	Answers
1	A B C D E F G H	21	A B C D E F G H
2	A B C D E F G H	22	A B C D E F G H
3	A B C D E F G H	23	A B C D E F G H
4	A B C D E F G H	24	A B C D E F G H
5	A B C D E F G H	25	A B C D E F G H
6	A B C D E F G H	26	A B C D E F G H
7	A B C D E F G H	27	A B C D E F G H
8	A B C D E F G H	28	A B C D E F G H
9	A B C D E F G H	29	A B C D E F G H
10	A B C D E F G H	30	A B C D E F G H
11	A B C D E F G H	31	A B C D E F G H
12	A B C D E F G H	32	A B C D E F G H
13	A B C D E F G H	33	A B C D E F G H
14	A B C D E F G H	34	A B C D E F G H
15	A B C D E F G H	35	A B C D E F G H
16	A B C D E F G H	36	A B C D E F G H
17	A B C D E F G H	37	A B C D E F G H
18	A B C D E F G H	38	A B C D E F G H
19	A B C D E F G H	39	A B C D E F G H
20	A B C D E F G H	40	A B C D E F G H

© UCLES 2010 Photocopiable

Sample answer sheet: Paper 3

Sample answer sheet: Paper 3

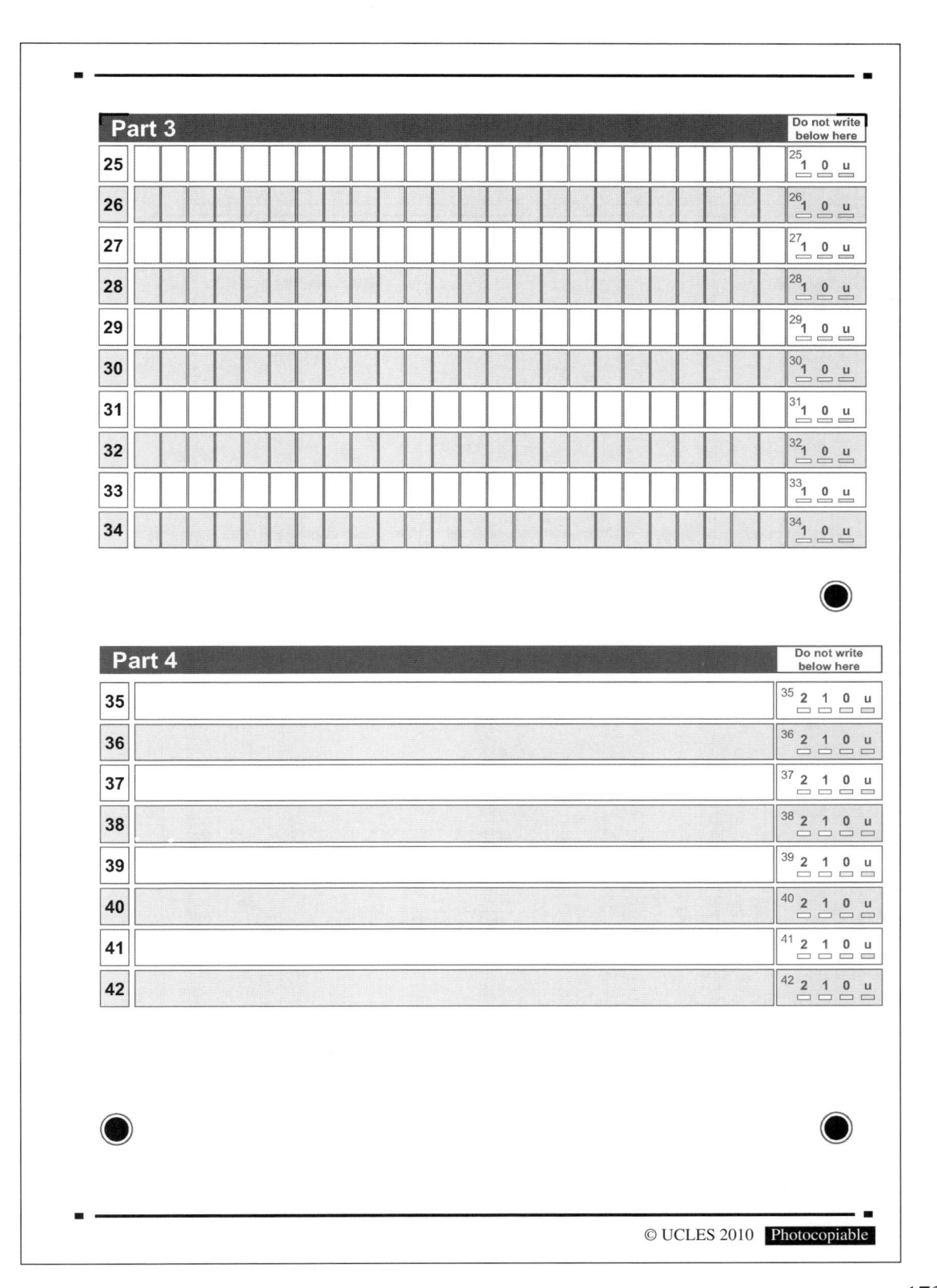

Part 3

	Do not write below here
25	25 1 0 u
26	26 1 0 u
27	27 1 0 u
28	28 1 0 u
29	29 1 0 u
30	30 1 0 u
31	31 1 0 u
32	32 1 0 u
33	33 1 0 u
34	34 1 0 u

Part 4

	Do not write below here
35	35 2 1 0 u
36	36 2 1 0 u
37	37 2 1 0 u
38	38 2 1 0 u
39	39 2 1 0 u
40	40 2 1 0 u
41	41 2 1 0 u
42	42 2 1 0 u

© UCLES 2010 Photocopiable

Sample answer sheet: Paper 4

UNIVERSITY of CAMBRIDGE
ESOL Examinations

SAMPLE

Candidate Name
If not already printed, write name in CAPITALS and complete the Candidate No. grid (in pencil).

Candidate Signature

Examination Title

Centre

Supervisor:
If the candidate is ABSENT or has WITHDRAWN shade here

Centre No.

Candidate No.

Examination Details

Test version: A B C D E F J K L M N   Special arrangements: S H

Candidate Answer Sheet

Instructions

Use a PENCIL (B or HB).
Rub out any answer you wish to change using an eraser.

Parts 1, 3 and 4:
Mark ONE letter for each question.

For example, if you think **B** is the right answer to the question, mark your answer sheet like this:

Part 2:
Write your answer clearly in CAPITAL LETTERS.

Write one letter or number in each box.
If the answer has more than one word, leave one box empty between words.

For example:

| 0 | N | U | M | B | E | R | | 1 | 2 | | | |

Turn this sheet over to start.

© UCLES 2010 Photocopiable

Sample answer sheet: Paper 4